William Loughton Smith

The Pretensions of Thomas Jefferson to the Presidency Examined

William Loughton Smith

The Pretensions of Thomas Jefferson to the Presidency Examined

ISBN/EAN: 9783337395759

Printed in Europe, USA, Canada, Australia, Japan

Cover: Foto ©ninafisch / pixelio.de

More available books at **www.hansebooks.com**

THE

PRETENSIONS OF

THOMAS JEFFERSON

TO THE

P R E S I D E N C Y

EXAMINED;

AND THE

CHARGES AGAINST

JOHN ADAMS

REFUTED.

ADDRESSED TO THE CITIZENS OF AMERICA IN GENERAL,

AND PARTICULARLY TO THE

ELECTORS

OF THE

P R E S I D E N T.

UNITED STATES, *October* 1796.

A WRITER under the fignature of Hampden, in the Richmond paper of the 1ft inftant, after afferting the exclufive right of Virginia to fill the office of Prefident, calls the attention of the citizens of that ftate to the illuftrious Thomas Jefferfon, as the fitteft character in the union to fill the Prefident's chair, and proceeds to enumerate the various pretenfions of that gentleman. They are,

1ft. His merits as a *philofopher.*

2d. As a *republican.*

3d. As a friend to the civil and religious rights of mankind.

4th. As a citizen who was in favor of the prefent federal government, but wifhed for amendments.

5th. As an enthufiaftic admirer of the French Revolution, without however furrendering the independency and felf-government of America.

6th. As a citizen, who had a proper fenfe of the perfidious conduct of Britain towards us, which he would have counteracted by *pacific* meafures, and meafures more advantageous than thofe which have taken place.

7th. As a citizen whofe diplomatic talents, and *political fagacity* are not inferior to his republicanifm and unalterable attachment to liberty.

8th. As poffeffing a *fortune* no lefs independent than his principles, and with a difpofition, continually impelling his *fertile* genius to difcoveries and improvements in the arts and fciences.

I shall not ftop to confider the exclufive claim of Virginia to the prefidency, but fhall proceed to examine the pretenfions of Thomas Jefferfon, as the above detailed. We may juftly prefume that his panegyrift has brought forward every title which this candidate poffeffes to the public favor on this occafion, and we may therefore fafely pronounce that thofe, and thofe alone, are the titles on which his pretenfions reft. I fhall examine,

1ft. The merit of T. Jefferfon, as a *philofopher.*

Whether a *moral* or a *natural* philofopher, or both, is not ftated by Hampden. The character of a good *moral* philofophcr is certainly a very respectable one, and if Mr. Jefferson's panegyrists can produce any evidence of his merits in that relation, I shall be happy to see them. If it can be shewn that he has disapproved of the *cruelties* which have stained the French revolution, that he has reprobated, instead of countenancing, the *impious doctrines* of Thomas Paine, that he has been an advocate for *peace; order* and submission to the laws, that he has never recommended in a public character, a profligate violation of public faith, in that case, his qualities as a good *moral* philosopher, would be valuable ingredients in the character of President of the United States.

WHETHER or not he has vindicated, the horrors and cruelties perpetrated in France, has been the advocate of *Thomas Paine* and the patron of his works, has fostered dissentions in the administration of the federal government, has connived at the opposition to the laws, has recommended measures destructive of the public credit and reputation, will hereafter appear by a review of his conduct, and by a reference to public facts and documents.

- IF Hampden only intended to exhibit him in the character of a great *natural philosopher*, I am at a loss to discern in what respects his merits as a natural philosopher, can recommend him to the presidency. It should seem that the active, anxious and responsible station of president would illy suit the calm, retired and exploring views of a *natural philosopher*, his merits might entitle him to the professorship of a college, but they would be as incompatible with the duties of the presidency as with the command of the Western army. As well might we have brought forward the eminent talents of Rittenhouse, had he been living, or the wonderful genius of Cox, the great bridge builder : indeed the merits of the famous *equestrian* Ricketts would have been at least as likely to recommend him to a station, which may occasionally require great military talents.

HAD Hampden justly appreciated the talents of this great natural philosopher, he would have continued him in his philosophical retirement, *employing his fertile genius in discoveries and improvements in the useful arts*, impaling butterflies and insects, and contriving turn-about chairs, *for the benefit of his fellow citizens and mankind in general*. While in the innocent enjoyment of such harmless occupations, no real friend to his peace and repose, and to the welfare of mankind, would draw this calm philosopher from such useful pursuits, to plunge him into the busy and dangerous vortex of an arduous station.

To be serious, let us examine the claim which his panegyrist sets up for him to the title of *philosopher*.

For the proof of his affertion, he refers us to the *Notes on Virginia*. As a moral philofopher, I do not recollect any part of that work, which juftifies the affertion ; but as a *natural* philofopher, his claim is probably founded on his ingenious differtation refpecting the primary caufes of difference between the whites and the blacks. It is worthy of infertion, and will furnifh an accurate idea of his philofophical fagacity. This philofopher had once formed the extravagant project of *emancipating all the flaves of Virginia*, and the more extravagant one of afterwards *fhipping them off* to fome other country ; in page 147 of his Notes on Virginia, he fays,—" it will probably be afked, " why not retain and incorporate the blacks in this ftate ? I " anfwer, deep rooted prejudices entertained by the whites, " ten thoufand recollections by the blacks of the *injuries* they " have fuftained, new provocations, *the real diftinctions which* " NATURE *has made*, and many other circumftances, will divide " us into parties and produce convulfions, which will never end " but in the extermination of the *one or the other race*. To thefe " objections, which are *political*, may be added others, which " are *phyfical and moral*. The firft difference which ftrikes us " is that of colour ; whether the black of the negro refides in " the reticular membrane between the fkin and the fcarf fkin, " or in the fcarf fkin itfelf, whether it proceeds from the colour " of the blood, or the colour of the bile, or from that of fome " other fecretion, *the difference is fixed in nature*, and is as *real* as " if its feat and caufe were better known to us. *And is this dif-* " *ference of no importance ?* Is it not the foundation of a greater " or a lefs fhare of beauty *in the two races ?* Are not the fine " mixtures of red and white, the expreffions of every paffion by " greater or lefs fuffufion of colour in the one, preferable to that " eternal monotony which reigns in the countenances, that im- " moveable veil of black which covers all the emotions of *the* " *other race ?* Add to thefe, flowing hair, a more elegant fym- " metry of form, their own judgment in favor of the whites, " declared by their preference of them as uniformly as is *the* " *preference of the oran outang for the black women over thofe of* " *his own fpecies.* Befides thofe of colour, figure and hair, there " are other *phyfical* diftinctions *proving a difference of race* ; they " have *lefs hair* on the face and *body*, they *fecrete lefs by the kidnies* " *and more by the glands of the fkin, which gives them a very* " *ftrong and difagreeable odour.* They are more tolerant of heat, " and lefs fo of cold, than the whites, perhaps *owing to a diffe-* " *rence of ftructure in the pulmonary apparatus* ; they are *more ar-* " *dent after their female* ; their griefs are tranfient ; in general " their exiftence appears to participate more of *fenfation* than " reflection. They are *in reafon* much *inferior to the whites*. It " is not againft experience to fuppofe that *different fpecies of the*

" *fame genus, or varieties of the fame fpecies,* may poffefs different
" qualifications. Will not a *lover of natural hiftory,* then, one
" who views the *gradations* in *all the races of animals,* with the
" *eye of philofophy,* excufe an effort to keep thofe in the depart-
" ment of man as *diftinct as nature has formed them* ; this unfor-
" tunate difference of colour, and *perhaps* of faculty, is *a power-*
" *ful obftacle to the emancipation of thefe people.* Many of their
" advocates while they wifh to *vindicate the liberty of human*
" *nature* are anxious alfo to *preferve its dignity and beauty.* Some
" of thefe, embarraffed by the queftion, what further is to be
" done with them, join themfelves in oppofition with thofe who
" are *actuated by fordid avarice only.* Among the Romans,
" emancipation required but one effort : the flave when made
" free might mix *without ftaining the blood of his mafter,* but *with*
" *us, a fecond is neceffary, unknown to hiftory ; when freed, he is*
" *to be removed beyond the reach of mixture.*"

A few comments on the foregoing very ridiculous and elaborate attempt to prove that the *negroes are an inferior race of
animals,* will place in a juft light the *philofophical* merits of the
author : This paffage has been felected, becaufe it is among
thofe which have been moft admired by the author's friends.

Firft, we obferve an affected anxiety to emancipate the negroes of Virginia, why ? " in order to vindicate the *liberty* of
the human race ;" but this commendable zeal prefently yields
to a more interefting anxiety " to preferve the *beauty* of the human race."

To extricate himfelf from the embarraffment into which he
is thrown by the conflicting defires of " vindicating the liberty
of the human race," and " preferving its beauty," he hits on
the notable expedient of emancipating all the flaves of Virginia, and then inftantly *fhipping them off,* like a herd of *black
cattle,* the Lord knows where. The defire of preferving the
beauty of the human race predominates, however, in the mind
of our philofopher ; for notwithftanding the flaves are to enjoy
a momentary freedom, they are fuddenly after to be feized,
bound, packed on board veffels, and againft their confent ex-
ported to fome lefs friendly regions, where they would be all
murdered or reduced to a more wretched ftate of flavery.—
Such are the noble and *enlarged* views of *philofophical* politicians !
But fome juftification muft be given for the latter part of this
merciful project : It was neceffary therefore to prove that the
blacks, (whofe emancipation was requifite to vindicate the liberty of the *human race,*) were not in fact of the *human race,*
for this muft be the author's meaning, if there be any meaning
in his work ; the idea of two or more human races, a black hu

man race, and a white human race, being too abfurd even for
him to have fuggefted ; it is true, his expreffions are fo vague
and contradictory, that it is difficult to afcertain very precifely
his meaning ; but taking the whole together, it refults in this,
that the blacks are a peculiar race of animals below *man* and
above the *oran outang*, a kind of *tertium quid*, a higher kind of
brute, hitherto undefcribed. I am at a lofs to annex any other
refult to the following expreffions and obfervations, viz. " The
real diftinctions which nature has made"—a difference in the
two races"—comparing the preference which the blacks have
for the whites " to the preference of the *oran outang* for the *black
women*"—fecreting lefs by the kidnies, and more by the glands
of the fkin than the whites—difference of ftructure in the pulmonary apparatus—being in *reafon* much inferior to the whites
—different fpecies of the fame genus, or varieties of the fame
fpecies—their exiftence participating more of *fenfation* than reflection—gradations in the *different races* of animals," &c.

THE confufion of ideas which pervaded the underftanding of
our author through the whole of this very ingenious and learned differtation muft be manifeft. At one moment he is anxious to emancipate the blacks, to *vindicate the liberty of the human race*—at another, he difcovers that the blacks are of a *different race* from the *human race*, and therefore when emancipated, muft be inftantly *removed* beyond the reach of mixture, leaft
he (or fhe) fhould *ftain the blood* of his (or her) mafter; not
recollecting what, from his fituation and other circumftances, he
ought to have recollected—that this *mixture* may take place
while the negro remains in flavery : he muft have feen all a-
round him fufficient marks of this *ftaining of blood* to have been
convinced that retaining them in flavery would not prevent it ;
he muft have been fatisfied that the mixture would not be the
lefs degrading from the *emancipated* ftate of the black. At a-
nother moment he difcovers that the blacks are indeed a part of
the human race, but then they are a *different fpecies* of the fame
genus, or they and the whites conftitute varieties of the fame
fpecies. In one place he afferts with confidence " that they
are *in reafon much inferior* to the whites ;" in another, he feems
to doubt it ; " this difference of colour, and *perhaps* of *faculty ;*" to juftify the *emancipation* of the blacks, they are made a
part of the human race; to juftify their *tranfportation* they are
claffed with the brutes.

But the moft extraordinary of all the felf contradictions of
this philofopher is found in a *Letter* written, while fecretary of
ftate, to a *Negro* named *Benjamin Banneker*, which letter, having a clofe relation to this fubject, may very properly be here
introduced.

We have feen from the above quotation, that our author was decidedly of opinion—1ft, That there was a *fixed difference in nature* between the whites and blacks—2d, That this amounted to a diftinction, conftituting the blacks a *differe t race*—3d, That the blacks were *in reafon much inferior* to the whites; their exiftence participating more of *fenfation* than reflection—4th, That this *inferiority* was evidently not produced by their *condition*, but *by nature.*

The negro Benjamin was the *reputed* author of an Almanac, which was either dedicated to, or fent, with fome complimentary epiftle, to his brother author, our philofopher, whofe philofophy was of fo pliant a quality, that, inftantly forgetting all his learned difcoveries on the fkin and fcarf fkin and kidnies of the unfavory Africans, he fat down and wrote to brother Benjamin a fraternizing epiftle, in which "he rejoiced to find that "NATURE had given to his *black brethren* talents equal to "thofe of *other colours,* and that the *appearance* of a want of "them, was owing *merely* to the *degraded condition* of their ex-"iftence, both in Africa and America." He then adds his *wifhes* for the emancipation of the negroes in the United States, as faft as circumftances will admit. Here we find a *direct and flat contradiction* to all his affertions on this fubject in his *Notes;* from which we muft infer, either that that work was compiled with fo much inaccuracy, and fuch want of information or reflection, that the moft trivial circumftance was fufficient to induce him to contradict its contents *himfelf;* or that he was fo influenced by a *ridiculous vanity,* fo tickled by a filly compliment from an "*unfavory animal of an inferior race,*" as wilfully and publicly to contradict, without any fhame or regard to public decency, his former affertions, ftill believing them to be well founded. His panegyrift may choofe from the above alternatives, that which may be the leaft injurious to his friend. He will probably attempt to vindicate the philofopher by introducing his candor which led him to recant an error. The wonderful production of Brother Benjamin, he will fay, had convinced him of the untruth of his former doctrine. But this apology will not do; becaufe the *Notes on Virginia* prove, that our philofopher had feen the *reputed* works of *other blacks,* at leaft *equal* in merit to Brother Benjamin's, and had fuggefted, that they were the production of fome white perfon, falfely attributed to the negroes. He had fully confidered and difcuffed this fubject: this appears from the preceding quotation; but to leave no room for doubt on this point, a further quotation fhall be inferted. Our author, in his great zeal to fupport his doctrine of the *inferiority of the race of the blacks,* proceeds thus to the proof: "They are *in reafon much inferior* to the whites;

" as, I think, one could fcarcely be found capable of tracing
" and comprehending the invefligations of Euclid ; in imagi-
" nation, they are dull, taftelefs and anomalous. Many have
" been brought up to the handicraft arts ; fome have been li-
" berally educated ; and all (in America) have lived in coun-
" tries where the arts and fciences are cultivated to a confidera-
" ble degree, and had before their eyes famples of the beft
" works from abroad. The *Indians*, with no advantages of
" this kind, will often carve figures on their pipes, not defti-
" tute of defign and merit ; they will crayon out an animal, a
" plant, or a country, fo as to prove the exiftence of a germ
" in their minds, which only wants cultivation. They afton-
" ifh you with ftrokes of the moft fublime oratory, fuch as
" prove their reafon and fentiment ftrong, their imagination
" glowing and elevated ; but *never* yet could I find that a
" *black* had uttered a thought above the level of plain narra-
" tion—never fee even an elementary trait of painting and
" fculpture. Love is the peculiar œftrum of the poet : their
" love is ardent, but it kindles the *fenfe* only, not the imagin-
" ation. Religion, indeed, has produced a *Phillis Wheatly*,
" but it could not produce a poet. The compofitions pub-
" lifhed *under her name*, are below the dignity of criticifm.
" *Ignatius Sancho* has approached nearer to merit in his com-
" pofition : Though we admit him to the firft place among
" thofe of his own colour, who have prefented themfelves to
" the public judgment, yet, when we compare him with the
" writers of the race among whom he lived, and particularly
" with the epiftolarly clafs, in which he has taken his own
" ftand, we are compelled to enroll him *at the bottom of the co-*
" *lumn.* This criticifm fuppofes the letters publifhed under
" his name, to be *genuine*, and to have received *amendment* from
" no other hand, *points which would not be eafy of invefligation,*
" (furprifing the fame reflections did not occur refpecting Ben-
" jamin, the almanac-maker !) The *improvement* of the blacks,
" in *body* and *mind*, in the *firft inftance* of their *mixture* with the
" *whites*, has been obferved by every one, *and proves, that their*
" *inferiority is not the effect merely of their condition of life.* A-
" mong the Romans, their *flaves* were often their *rareft ar-*
" *tifts;* they excelled too in fcience, infomuch as to be ufually
" employed as tutors to their mafter's children. Epictetus,
" Terence and Phœdrus were flaves ; *but they were of the race*
" *of whites. It is not their condition, then, but* NATURE, *which*
" *has produced the diftinction.*"

FROM the above it is evident, that he had well examined
this fubject, and that his direct and grofs contradiction of all
this doctrine, fo foon after, fprung principally from a wifh to

acquire a little popularity with the free negroes. What muſt we now think of a philoſopher, who, in one publication, aſſerts it to be *"proved,* that the inferiority of the blacks is not " the effect merely of their *condition* of life, but a *diſtinction of* " *race,* produced by *nature ;"* and in another " that it is ow- " ing *merely* to the degraded *condition* of their exiſtence." Did he flatter himſelf that his letter to Banneker would eſcape publication, and only be handed round among the free negroes, who probably never had read his *Notes,* or if they had, would forgive the paſt injury, on account of the preſent recantation? Did he hope thus to eſcape detection, and thus artfully to ob- tain the character of a great and ſagacious philoſopher with the friends of negro ſlavery, while he would be rewarded with the plaudits of the abolition ſocieties and free negroes?—What ſhall we think of a *ſecretary of ſtate* thus *fraternizing* with ne- groes, writing them complimentary epiſtles, ſtiling them *his black brethren,* congratulating them on the evidences of their *genius,* and aſſuring them of his good wiſhes for their ſpeedy emancipation; what muſt the citizens of the *ſouthern ſtates,* particularly, whoſe ſlaves are guaranteed to them as *their pro- perty* by the conſtitution and laws of the United States, think of a *ſecretary of the United States,* (whoſe peculiar duty it was to watch over the intereſts of every part of the Union,) who, at the hazard of the primary intereſts of thoſe ſtates, promulgates his approbation of a ſpeedy emancipation of their ſlaves?— What will they think of ſuch a *candidate* for the office of pre- ſident of the United States?—What will they ſay to the *Elec- tors* of the *ſouthern ſtates* who ſhall be ſo *entirely regardleſs of the intereſts and future peace and tranquillity of their country* as to vote for ſuch a perſon? But this ſubject, from its importance, re- quires a further conſideration.

THOMAS JEFFERSON, ſecretary of ſtate of the United States, in his letter to the negro Banneker, acknowledges him- ſelf converted from all his former opinions, reſpecting the infe- riority of the black race, and declares himſelf convinced " that " *nature* has given to his *black brethren* talents *equal to thoſe of* " *other colours,* and that the *appearance* of a want of them is " owing *merely* to the *degraded condition* of their exiſtence both " in Africa and *America."* He concludes his fraternizing epiſ- tle with theſe words, " I can add with truth, that nobody " *wiſhes more ardently* to ſee a good ſyſtem commenced for " *raiſing* the *condition* both of their *body and mind* to *what it* . " *ought to be, as faſt* as the *imbecility* of their preſent exiſtence " and *other circumſtances* which cannot be neglected, will ad- mit!" Notwithſtanding the caution and *cunning* with which the latter ſentence is worded, to admit of a double interpreta-

tion, if neceſſary, it cannot be denied that, taking the whole
letter together, it meant to expreſs to the negro, Benjamin,
an ardent wiſh to ſee an early ſyſtem of *emancipation* in the
ſouthern ſtates ; he had juſt ſaid, that nature had given to his
black brethren talents *equal* to thoſe of the whites, and that the
appearance of a want of them was owing *merely* to their *degraded condition ;* he immediately adds *his ardent wiſh* for a good
ſyſtem for *raiſing the condition* both of their *body and mind* to
what it ought to be, that is, in plain Engliſh, " from the degraded condition of ſlavery to a ſtate of freedom." The qualification ſubjoined, viz. " As faſt as the *imbecility* of their
" preſent exiſtence, and *other circumſtances* which cannot be
" neglected, will admit," was introduced as an artful ſalvo,
not too far to commit himſelf ; behind theſe equivocal expreſſions he thought himſelf ſheltered from an attack in the ſouthern ſtates ; he might, if puſhed, conſtrue them into an opinion, that for centuries to come, emancipation would be impolitic and dangerous, becauſe *other circumſtances* would not juſtify the meaſure. But this is certain, that had he viewed the
meaſure of emancipation as a dangerous one, either he would
have diſcountenanced it, or at leaſt, on ſo delicate a ſubject,
kept ſilent. Why ſuch an anſwer to the negro's letter ? Why
not confine his anſwer merely to the almanac, and to the uſual
compliment on ſuch an occaſion ? Why make a *parade of his
opinion,* by extolling the natural genius of the blacks, remind-
ing them of their degraded condition and expreſſing a wiſh to
ſee it changed ? Either he was a friend to emancipation, or he
was not: if the former, then the qualification reſpecting *other circumſtances* was abſurd and unmeaning ; if the latter, then the encomiums on the talents of the blacks, and the ardent wiſh for
their releaſe from their degraded condition, were equally abſurd.
Again, he tells Banneker, and through him all the negroes in
America, " I am ſatisfied that your *natural talents* are *equal* to
" thoſe of the whites, and that the *appearance* of a want of
" them in you is owing *merely* to the *degraded condition* of your
exiſtence ;" now what does he mean by adding, " I wiſh to
" ſee you emancipated, as ſoon as the *imbecility* of your pre-
" ſent exiſtence will admit ?" If the appearance of their want
of talents was owing *merely* to their *condition,* the ſooner they
emerged from that condition the better ; if their imbecility was
produced ſolely by their condition, that imbecility would ceaſe
the moment they were emancipated ; what kind of reaſoning
is it, to charge their imbecility altogether to their condition,
and yet to expect an amelioration of their reaſon antecedently
to their change of condition ? It is no better than the blunder
of the *Iriſhman,* who would not ſuffer his ſon to go into the
water, until he could ſwim. According to our author's mode

of reasoning, the negroes could never be emancipated, his ardent wish could never be gratified; the slavery of the negroes he says is the sole cause of their imbecility; but he immediately adds, they must remain in slavery 'till their minds are enlightened. How are they to acquire this necessary pre-requisite to emancipation, when, according to his doctrine, that *pre-requisite* can only be obtained *after* emancipation? Here is such a jumble of ideas, such a confounding of *cause* and *effect* in this letter, that the production of it by a man of common understanding can only be accounted for by ascribing it to a pitiful grasp at popularity from a class which he had despised, and to an ardent wish for the emancipation of the southern negroes, shrouded in the cautious and ambiguous language of one, who thought the times not yet ripe enough for a *full disclosure* of his dangerous views.—Another qualification in his letter refers to " *other circumstances,* which cannot be neglected." What circumstances had he in view, to prevent the immediate emancipation of the blacks? Does he allude to the difficulties which would oppose his *transportation scheme?* Surely the negroes would not thank him for their liberty on such terms; but in his Notes on Virginia he is decidedly of opinion that the negroes of the United States, when freed, must be *removed* beyond the reach of mixture; rather a harsh treatment for his black brethren! Whence proceeds this right of transportation (without a crime or conviction) our philosopher has not informed us, and on what pretext of law or justice, freemen, not even charged with any offence, are to be shipped off, like cattle, I am unable to discover: had he proposed shipping them off, while slaves, there would be more sense in the project; but first to emancipate and invest them with all the rights of free citizens, and then forthwith to treat them as slaves and cattle, is altogether unintelligible.

PERHAPS the project was, to make it a preliminary condition *sine qua non* with the Africans, that they should be free, subject to immediate transportation: but when free, it is doubtful how many of them would consider themselves bound by such a condition; indeed it is questionable whether many of them would accept their freedom on such terms. But waving these difficulties, how impolitic would it not be to banish from the country several hundred thousand of our *black brethren, to whom nature has given talents equal to our own,* and who, in spite of their monotonous † colour and offensive secretions (circumstances common to thousands of other colours) might become very useful citizens, and, according to the secretary's letter, rank with the whites in

---

† Who ever heard, before Mr. Jefferson's time, of the *monotony of colours?*

point of genius and merit, at the very inftant of their emancipation.—If the fecretary of State meant in his letter to allude to his fhipping projeft by the words " other circumftances," it would have been but candid in him to have unfolded to his black brethren the whole extent of his views,
that they might be fully apprifed of the terms on which they
had his ardent wifhes for emancipation. Having omitted fo
effential a part of the plan, it is to be prefumed, that he has
abandoned it, and now wifhes for their emancipation *as faft as
other circumftances* will allow it to be accomplifhed ; that is, as
foon as he fhall find it convenient to difpofe of *his own*, and
as foon as the meafures which are now purfuing for that purpofe in feveral of the ftates, even in fome of the foutnern ftates,
and the principles which have been tranfplanted from the
French colonies into America, and *his* countenance *as Prefident of the United States*, fhall combine to make the meafure appear pradticable in the eyes of its promoters.

It appears almoft incredible (and could not be credited had
we not the fadts before our eyes) that the fame Thomas Jefferfon, who not many years ago publifhed to the world his opinion, " that there were powerful obftacles to the emancipation
" of the blacks, becaufe deep rooted prejudices entertained
" by the whites, ten thoufand recollections by the blacks of
" the *injuries* they have fuftained, new provocations, the real
" diftindtions which nature has made, and many other circum-
" ftances, will divide us into parties and produce *convulfions*
" which will never end but in the *extermination of the one or the
" other race*," fhould have recently declared *his ardent wifh for
fuch emancipation*, at the rifk of all the horrid confequences
which he had himfelf fo ftrongly depidted.

If fuch a wonderful change has been wrought in his mind,
to what are we to impute it ? I can find no other clue to it
than the delufive and vifionary principles which he has imbibed
on that fubjedt by his refidence in France. It is to be remarked that he publifhed his notes on Virginia, after fpending the
greateft part of his life in Virginia, among Negroe holders and
Negroes, and at a period when he muft be prefumed to be pretty well acquainted with Negroes, and aware of the confequences
of their emancipation ; he wrote his letter to Banneker, the
Negro, *foon after his return from France.*

If his fentiments on this fubjedt were not changed when
he wrote to the Negro, then his letter to him is a piece of
grofs hypocrify, calculated to filch a little popularity from a
few free Negroes, and the friends of emancipation, at the ex-
pence of his own charadter and of the peace of his country.

WHETHER the Secretary complied with the promife made in that letter to Banneker " of fending his almanac to the great philofopher *Condorcet*," as a teftimony of his black brother's extraordinary genius, we have never learnt.

MANY further fimilar illuftrations might be made of the ex-fecretary's *philofophical* talents from his *notes on Virginia* ; thefe may for the prefent fuffice. At a future opportunity, we may find leifure to notice his very extraordinary *penal code*, and his whimfical fyftem of *retaliation*, his *wife* attempt to refute the account of the *deluge*, (evidently ftated by Mofes to be a *miracle*) by a recurrence to philofophical and merely *natural* principles ; and fundry other philofophical abfurdities. His plagiary *report* on *weights and meafures* will be adverted to under another head.

AFTER thefe fpecimens of his talents, we may fafely venture to withhold from Thomas Jefferfon the title of philofopher.

BUT we fhould incur no danger in yielding to his claim in the fulleft extent, becaufe it muft be obvious to men of the fmalleft experience in public life, that of all beings, a philofopher, makes the worft politician; that if any one circumftance more than another, could difqualify Mr. Jefferfon for the Prefidency, it would be the charge of his being a philofopher. Not believing him to poffefs any thing more than the *mafk* of philofophy, *my* objection to his election would certainly not reft on that ground ; but as there may be fome, who, having read his works fuperficially, may have been deceived by that character, which is fometimes acquired, becaufe no one has been at the trouble to fcrutinize and ftrip it of its borrowed garb, to them I repeat that, admitting him to be a moft learned philofopher, fuch a character alone creates his difqualification for the Prefidency.

IN turning over the page of hiftory, we find it teeming with evidences of the ignorance and mifmanagement of philofophical politicians. The great *Locke* was employed to frame a conftitution for Carolina ; but it abounded fo much with regulations, inapplicable to the ftate of things for which it was defigned, fo full of *theoretic whimfies*, that it was foon thrown afide. *Condorcet*, a particular friend of our American philofopher, was a great French philofopher : his conftitution, propofed in 1793, contains more abfurdities than were ever before piled up in any fyftem of Government ; it was fo radically defective that its operation was never even attempted ; † Condorcet's political

† Hear what *Boiffy d'Anglas* fays of the Conftitution of *Condorcet*, a brother laborer in Philofophy and Politics of Thomas Jefferfon : meditated amidft intrigue and ambition, conceived in the bofom of vice, that Conftitution is nothing more than the *concentration of all the elements of diforder, and the organization of anarchy*. What indeed muft we think of a Conftitution, which organizes the partial infurrection of powers, independent of the conftituted authorities, and legalizes the reign of plunder and terror." Compare this, Americans, with the principles and practice of the Democratic Societies and the other fupporters of Thomas Jefferfon ! !

follies, and the wretched termination of his career are well known; he had philofophy enough to know how to raife a ftorm, but not enough to avert its effects. The affairs of France have fince been more ably conducted (except during the fhort ariftocracy of Robefpierre) by men who are good politicians, but fortunately for France, *not philofophers.*

RITTENHOUSE was a great philofopher, but the only proof we have had of *his political* talents was his fuffering himfelf to be wheedled into the *Prefidency* of the *Democratic Society* of Philadelphia, a fociety with which he was even afhamed to affociate, tho' cajoled and flattered into the *loan* of his *name.* Many other inftances might be adduced.

THE characteriftic traits of a philofopher, when he turns politician, are, timidity, whimficalnefs, a difpofition to reafon from certain principles, and not from the true nature of man; a pronenefs to predicate all his meafures on certain abftract theories, formed in the recefs of his cabinet, and not on the exifting ftate of things and circumftances; an inertnefs of mind, as applied to governmental policy, a wavering of difpofition when great and fudden emergencies demand promptnefs of decifion and energy of action. If the laws are oppofed and infurrection raifes its creft, the infurgents will always calculate on the weaknefs and indecifion of the executive (if a philofopher) and they will be juftified in their calculations, for he will hefitate till all is loft; he will be wandering in the labyrinths of philofophical fpeculations, moralizing on the fin of fpilling human blood, and foolifhly perfuading himfelf that mankind can *always* be reclaimed and brought back to their duty by *wholefome advice.* His mind will be conftantly attracted to his favorite purfuits; and his prefidential duties, will, of courfe, be poftponed to more pleafing avocations.

LET us fuppofe one of thefe exploring and profound philofophers elected Prefident of the United States, and a foreign minifter, on his firft introduction into his cabinet, furprifing him in the act of infpecting the *fkin and the fcarf fkin* of a *black and a white pig,* in order to difcover the caufes of difference which nature has created in their colour, or with the fame view anatomizing the kidnies and glands of a *Negro* to afcertain the *nature of his fecretions?* Would not the minifter's firft obfervation be, that the philofopher would be much better employed in his retirement at home, and his fecond, that fuch a Prefident would furnifh excellent materials for him to make ufe of.

WHAT refpect would the officers of government entertain for a prefident, whom they fhould find, on waiting on him for inftructions, bufily engaged in impaling a butterfly or contriving

with affiduous perfeverance an † *eafy chair* of new conftruction ?
Would not an attention to thefe littleneffes make him the ridi-
cule of the world ? The great *Washington* was, thank
God, no philofopher ; had *he* been one, we fhould never have
feen his great military exploits ; we fhould never have profpered
under his wife adminiftration. There is another characteriftic
trait in philofophers highly dangerous, namely, their extreme *o-
penmefs to flattery* ; a flatterer will be always fure to gain a philofopher's affections ; a philofophical prefident will be confequent-
ly moft influenced by *that nation which flatters moft* ; which that
is, need not be mentioned : if their agents do not fail in this
national qualification, fuch a prefident will be their moft devoted
fervant : he will alfo be perpetually furrounded by a fwarm of
domeftic flatterers ; and as they are generally the bafeft of characters, the companions he will be attached to, and the meafures
they will promote, may without difficulty be predicted.

But, although I have thus denied to Mr. Jefferfon the title
of a *real philofopher*, I am ready to allow that he poffeffes the
inferior characteriftics, and the *externals* of philofophy. By one,
ambitious of paffing with the world for a philofopher, the firft
were eafily acquired, the laft as eafily affumed. The inferior
characteriftics, as applied to the fcience of politics, are a want of
fteadinefs, a conftitutional indecifion and verfatility, vifionary,
wild and fpeculative fyftems, and various other defective features,
which have been already pourtrayed—Indeed fo unfettled is the
mind of a *would be* philofopher, fo capricious and verfatile are
the principles of thefe *philofophical mimics*, that they attempt to
reconcile the moft irreconcilable theories, and to juftify the moft
inconfiftent acts by the fame ftandard. Thus you will find thefe
pretenders to philofophy, at one moment, coolly juftifying the
moft atrocious and *fanguinary cruelties*, provided they are *means*
to a certain favorite *end* ; at another, cautioufly diffuading from
vigorous, tho' neceffary meafures, left they might fatally iffue
in the fhedding of human blood. *Condorcet* and *Briffot* were,
like Jefferfon, *reputed* philofophers ; they fet up certain wild
and mifchievous theories of government ; of courfe, followed
the emancipation of the negroes in the French Weft-Indies, and,
of courfe, the maffacre of the whites, and the defolation of the
colonies : this was reprefented to them, by a deputation from
the colonies, warning them of the fatal confequences of their
principles. What was *Philofopher Condorcet's* reply ? Attend
to it, Citizens of the fouthern States ! ! He anfwered with true
philofophic calmnefs, " *Perifh all the colonifts*, rather than that
we fhould deviate one tittle from our principles." This is the

---

† Who has not heard from the fecretary the praifes of his wonderful *Whirligig
Chair*, which had the miraculous quality of allowing the perfon feated in it to turn
his head, without moving his tail ? Who has not admired his fertile *genius* in the production of his *Epicurean fide-board*, and other Glafs Krackery?

enlightened Condorcet; to whom his friend Jefferson, ſtimulated by a ſympathetic philanthrophy, ſent Banneker's Almanac, as the higheſt proof of his admiration of the Negro's work. This is the *ſame Condorcet* who could, with calmneſs, ſee the colonies laid waſte, and thouſands of aged coloniſts and innocent women and children maſſacred, and yet was perpetually preaching up philanthropy and univerſal benevolence. *Briſſot* was much ſuch another character, and they both deſervedly met the ſame fate. .

As ignorant people are often impoſed upon by an appearance of philoſophy, thoſe, who have ambitious deſigns, readily aſſume its *externals*: theſe conſiſt in a ridiculous affectation of ſimplicity and humility, in a thouſand frivolities, and little puerile tricks, which always render the performer contemptible in the eyes of diſcerning people, who ſoon diſcover that under the aſſumed cloak of humility, lurks the moſt *ambitious ſpirit*, the moſt overweening pride and hauteur, and that the *externals* of ſimplicity and humility afford but a flimſy veil to the *internal* evidences of ariſtocratic ſplendor, ſenſuality and epicureaniſm.

Mr. Jefferson has been held up and characterized by his friends as " the quiet, modeſt retiring philoſopher—as the plain, ſimple, unambitious republican." He ſhall not now, for the firſt time, be regarded as the intriguing incendiary— the aſpiring turbulent competitor, unleſs facts ſhall warrant the ſuggeſtion : of theſe an enlightened public muſt judge.

What, if a quiet, modeſt, unambitious philoſopher, at a delicate criſis, withdrawing himſelf from a poſt of duty, from an alledged attachment to philoſophical purſuits, and a ſtrong antipathy to public honors, ſhould immediately devote his hours of retirement *to mature his ſchemes of concealed ambition*, and at the appointed time, come forth the undiſguiſed *candidate for the higheſt honors*, and for the moſt arduous ſtation to which ambition can aſpire ?

Would not *this trait* alone ſufficiently mark his character and his views ?

To ſome few of his fellow cittizens, this may perhaps be the *firſt time* his real character has been diſcovered ; but let *them* recollect that there is always " *a firſt time*," when characters, ſtudious of artful diſguiſes are unveiled, when the vizor of ſtoiciſm is plucked from the brow of the epicurean, when the plain garb of quaker ſimplicity is ſtripped from the concealed voluptuary, when *Cæſar, coyly refuſing* the proffered diadem, is found to be Cæſar *rejecting* the trappings, " but tenaciouſly *graſping* the *ſubſtance* of imperial domination."

C

The pretensions of Thomas Jefferson to the Presidency, in the relation of a *philosopher*, having been canvassed, we shall next proceed to examine his pretensions as " a *republican*, and a friend to the civil and religious rights of his fellow-citizens."

The observations already made, respecting the assumption of the *externals* of *philosophy*, will apply with peculiar force to the assumption of the *externals* of *republicanism*. There are *impostors* in *patriotism* as well as in philosophy ; and as the former are the most dangerous, so ought we the more carefully to be on our guard against them. It is now become so common a trick in France, in England, and in the United States, for every ambitious demagogue to put on the *garb* of *patriotism*, to vociferate in the *language* of *liberty*, that every prudent and intelligent citizen immediately suspects them of some mischievous design ; and these suspicions have been warranted by fatal experience.—Who wore the externals of republicanism, who spoke the language of liberty more than *Marat* and *Robespierre* ? Who was a greater friend to the civil and religious rights of his fellow-citizens than Cromwell ? Who bellowed more for liberty than the insurgent and fugitive *Bradford* ? In France, the actors in the late insurrection against the government, not content with the title of *patriots*, arrogantly stiled themselves the EXCLUSIVE PATRIOTS. In short, read but a few pages of ancient or modern history, inspect but a few columns of a newspaper, and you will find, that every aspiring, turbulent, and seditious demagogue, has always begun by assuming the externals of patriotism, and vociferating in the language of liberty, as a cloak and an aid to his nefarious projects.

WHENEVER I hear a man make a parade of his own republicanism, or his patriotism, or his overflowing zeal for his country's good, I instantly inquire, whether he is a candidate for office ? When his puffers proclaim his republican virtues, and his love of country, I inquire into his *past conduct* : *that* is the true *test* of patriotism. Republicanism (that much abused word) is discovered by opinions, not by professions. Patriotism announces itself by DEEDS, not by words. When WASHINGTON was *unanimously* called to the Presidency, he required no *puffing*, no *Hampdens* to blazon his fame. His past conduct, his genuine merit, his long services, were recorded in every breast. He required no affected retirement, no pretended philosophy, no coyish rejection of public honors, no deep planned machinery to bring *him* forth to public notice. And whenever the *public eye* of America shall fix itself on a prominent object, it will have been attracted to it by well-known virtues, and well-tried abilities ; not by the artificial parade of arrogant pretensions, or the deceptive puffings of interested intriguers.

HAMPDEN, in bringing forward Mr. Jefferſon's *republicaniſm* as a title to public favor, could not have ſeriouſly intended this very common and univerſal qualification as a mark of any peculiar merit : It is to be preſumed we are *all republicans*. I have mixed a great deal with the world ; I have viſited every part of the Union ; I have heard the political ſentiments of every deſcription of people—and I can with truth, and moſt ſolemnly, aver, that I have never met with a citizen of the United States, who expreſſed a wiſh for any other form of government for the United States, than the *republican*.

YET I am aware that Hampden, in ſpecifying this qualification, among others, meant leſs to point at the poſſeſſion of it by Mr. Jefferſon, than at the ſuppoſed want of it in his competitor, Mr. Adams.

IT is well known, that one of the *tricks of party* employed by Mr. Jefferſon and his adherents, has been to repreſent that worthy citizen, Mr. Adams, as a friend to monarchy and privileged orders. It is obſerved by our experienced *Preſident*, in his late excellent addreſs, " that one of the expedients of par-
" ty, to acquire influence with particular diſtricts, is, to miſ-
" repreſent the opinions and aims of other diſtricts." So, one of the expedients of Mr. Jefferſon's party, to acquire influence with the people, who are republicans, is, to miſrepreſent the opinions of their competitors and opponents, as being *anti-republican.*

WITH the vain hope of impreſſing this opinion, reſpecting Mr. Adams, on the public mind, various paſſages have been *garbled* from his work, entitled, " A *Defence* of the *American Conſtitutions ;*" a book expreſsly written for the purpoſe of *vindicating thoſe conſtitutions* from the ſtrictures of monſieur Turgot, a French theoriſt, who condemned the ſeparation of the American legiſlatures into two branches. The object of Mr. Adams was, to ſhew the abſolute neceſſity, in a republican government, of checks and balances ; and that veſting all the legiſlative power in *a ſingle body*, had, at all times, and in all republican governments, ended in the ſlavery of the people. To prove this, he refers to all the ancient and modern republics ; and neceſſarily introduces the various checks and balances which had been deviſed in each, or for the want of which the people had loſt their liberties.

THIS is called by Hampden, and other ſycophants of Mr. Jefferſon, " an elaborate book in favour of privileged orders,
" and of a plan of government, compounded of a ſufficient
" mixture of monarchy."

NOTHING is more falfe than this affertion. The book is in favour of diftributing the legiflative power in the United States, into two branches : and fo much good fenfe and found reafoning does it contain, that, for the honour of Mr. Adams, every conftitution which has been made in the United States fince his work has been fo organized.——That of Pennfylvania, which had always been conftructed on the plan of a fingle branch, was, in 1790, a few years after Mr. Adams's work appeared, changed, and organized with two branches ;—a change effected almoft unanimoufly in their convention, and allowed to be productive of the moft effential advantages.

IF this *party* have fucceeded in fome quarters of the Union, where the means of information have been limited, how have they effected their bafe purpofes ? By garbling detached fentences of Mr. Adams's book, and mifreprefenting his opinions.

THERE is no publication in the world which may not be condemned by this unfair mode of proceeding. When an individual is profecuted for publifhing a *libel* even in England, although the charge is founded on certain paffages, extracted from the work, the judge always charges the jury to *read the whole work*, and to ground their verdict on *the whole, taken together ;* the jury carry out the book and read the whole of it, before they undertake to condemn the author. Yet Hampden, probably himfelf a fprig of the law, and who, I'll venture to fay, has never read the book he condemns, calls on the enlightened and liberal citizens of America to pafs perpetual fentence of condemnation on Mr. Adams, (whom he allows to have been *a patriot of* 1776) on the ftrength of a few broken and detached fentences.

JUDGE WILSON, in the convention of Pennfylvania, when the federal conftitution was under difcuffion, made the following reply to fome of its opponents : " Take *detached parts* of any fyftem whatever, in the manner thefe gentlemen have hitherto taken this conftitution, and you will make it abfurd and inconfiftent with itfelf. I do not confine this obfervation to human performances alone : it will apply to divine writings. An anecdote, which I have heard, exemplifies this obfervation : When Sternhold's and Hopkins' verfions of the Pfalms was ufually fung in churches, a line was firft read by the clerk, and then fung by the congregation. A failor had ftepped in, and heard the clerk read this line—

" The Lord will come, and he will not——"

The failor ftared ; but when the clerk read the next line,

" Keep filence, but fpeak out,———"

the failor left the church, convinced the people were not in their fenfes.

" This ftory, added Mr. Wilfon, may convey an idea of the treatment of the plan before you ; although it contains found fenfe, when conneɕted, yet by the detached manner of confidering it, it appears highly abfurd."

The paffages, which have been feleɕted from Mr. Adams's book by his enemies, are generally *narratives* concerning the forms of government of other countries, in which there exift-ed a monarchy or privileged orders, and the defeɕts of which he adduces as illuftrations of his fyftem in favor of a *balanced republican government*. When he fpeaks of the United States[†] he exprefsly rejoices at our happinefs, " *becaufe* OUR PEOPLE *are fovereign, and becaufe we have* NO HEREDITARY *titles, honors, offices, nor diftinɕtions.*' It would have been fingular indeed had he fet out with writing a book *in defence of the American conftitutions*, and then publifhed a panegyric on a fyftem, direɕt-ly oppofed to thofe conftitutions : And yet this grofs abfurdity is alledged by his opponents.

BUT to place beyond a doubt the impreffion which this book, (fo much reviled by our jacobins) has made on the difin-terefted, candid and enlightened, not only of our own, but of other nations, I will refer to the fpeech of *Boiffy d' Anglas*, one of the pureft republicans in France, in the convention, on difcuffing their prefent conftitution. All France had juft at that moment fworn eternal hatred to monarchy and privileged orders ; any encomiums therefore on an author fuppofed to be friendly to monarchy and privileged orders, would not have been favorably received ; Mr. Adams's book had been tranf-lated into the French language, had been much read by that nation, and was well known : Boiffy d'Anglas declared, in the convention, that " the committee who had drawn up the conftitution, were much indebted to the EXCELLENT WORK of that celebrated American patriot, JOHN ADAMS, for many of the LIGHTS they had acquired on the fubjeɕt of true REPUBLICAN government." Such was the opinion formed of Mr. Adams's book by thofe who had no *perfonal intereft* in at-tempting to difparage the work or its author.

MR. ADAMS's work, which has furnifhed fuch a handle for the malignant criticifms of his adverfaries, and of thofe who dread his juft pretenfions to the public gratitude, was

† *See* Defence of the American Conftitutions, page 95.

written in the year 1786. Yet we heard little of his alledged monarchical principles till about the year 1791. This will be hereafter accounted for. It is very certain that Mr. *Jefferson* himself did not, in the year 1789, three years after the work was written, fufpect Mr. Adams of foftering any fuch principles ; for we find in a letter ‡ from Mr. Jefferfon, dated Paris, March 15, 1789, thefe expreffions : " I know " there are fome among us who would now eftablifh a mo- " narchy, but they are *inconfiderable* in number and *weight of* " *character*." No one will doubt that Mr. Jefferfon had then feen Mr. Adams's book ; the intimacy which had long fub- fifted between thofe characters, the curiofity of the former on literary and particularly on political fubjects, his fituation as the minifter of the United States at a court, and among learn- ed men, at that time particularly inquifitive on fuch fubjects, where fuch a work would be neceffarily an interefting and ge- neral topic of converfation, and the high character of the lat- ter, then a minifter at a neighbouring court, are all circumftan- ces which muft remove every doubt of the fact.

As little doubt can there be that at the time Mr. Jefferfon wrote the letter referred to, he did not confider Mr. Adams as a perfon *inconfiderable in weight of character.* Thence it is clear that although Mr. Jefferfon had read Mr. Adams's book in 1789, he did not then infer from it that the author was a friend to monarchy, for had he drawn fuch a conclufion, he could not have faid, with truth, that the friends of monarchy were inconfiderable in weight of character. What afterwards led to the difcovery that Mr. Adams was a favorer of monar- chy, is now to be unfolded.

In the fummer of 1790, the Prefident was afflicted with an alarming diforder which threatened his life. Already a fuc- ceffor was talked of ; various candidates prefented themfelves to the public mind, and among them the Vice-Prefident ftood moft confpicuous. It inftantly became the fyftematic policy of Mr. Jefferfon and his adherents, to ruin in the public efti- mation a formidable rival, by charging the Vice-Prefident with an attachment to monarchy and privileged orders.

About that time, Mr. Jefferfon, being fecretary of ftate, conferred a *finecure* office in his department with a falary of two hundred and fifty dollars a year on Mr. Freneau, to induce him to remove to Philadelphia, and fet up a newfpaper at the feat of government, called the *National Gazette.* This paper

‡ This letter and fome others, fuppofed to be written to Mr. Madifon, on the fub- ject of the new conftitution of the United States, were publifhed in Dunlap's paper in 1792, to prove (what they did not) Mr. Jefferfon's approbation of that conftitution.

forthwith teemed with the moſt illiberal abuſe of Mr. Adams, and twice a week regularly rung the changes againſt his ſyſtem of monarchy and privileged orders.

But, to give more éclat and charaſter to the charge, the ſecretary of ſtate himſelf, who only, two years before, had not diſcovered any thing injurious to the public weal in Mr. Adams's book, did not diſdain to appear in print, and commence the attack.

The firſt volume of Thomas Paine's " Rights of Man," made its appearance ; the opportunity was eagerly ſeized, to anſwer the double purpoſe of wounding a competitor, and of laying in an additional ſtock of popularity, by aſſociating and circulating the name of Thomas Jefferſon with a popular production of a once favorite writer, on a favorite ſubjeſt.

For this purpoſe, the ſecretary of ſtate wrote an epiſtle to a printer in Philadelphia, tranſmitting the work for republication, and containing the following paſſage : " I am extreme-" ly pleaſed to find it will be reprinted here, and that ſome-" thing is at length to be publicly ſaid againſt the *political he-*" *reſies* which have ſprung up among us. I have no doubt " our citizens will *rally* a ſecond time round the *ſtandard* of " common ſenſe."

There was not a man in the United States acquainted with the inſinuations which had been propagated againſt Mr. Adams, who did not inſtantly apply the remark ; and the ſignal was ſo well underſtood by the partizans of the writer, that a general attack immediately commenced.

The National Gazette of *Freneau*, faithful to its *duty*, and the newſpapers of the *party* in the different ſtates, reſounded with invective and ſcurrility againſt the patriot, who was thus marked out as *the objeſt of perſecution.*

But it was quickly perceived that diſcerning and reſpecta-ble men diſapproved of the ſtep which the ſecretary had tak-en. It was of conſequence to endeavour to maintain their good opinion. Inſincere proteſtations and excuſes, as frivo-lous as aukward, were multiplied by the ſecretary to veil the real deſign. " The gentleman alluded to," he proteſted, " never once entered his mind ; it was never imagined that the " printer would be ſo *incautious* as to publiſh the letter. No-" thing more had been in view, than to turn a handſome pe-" riod, and avoid the *baldneſs* of a note, that did nothing but " preſent the compliments of the writer ! "

Thus, a ſolemn invocation to the people of America, on a

moſt ſerious and important ſubject, dwindled at once into a brilliant conceit that tickled the imagination too much to be reſiſted. The imputation of *levity* .was preferred to that of malice.

But when the people of America preſented themſelves to the diſturbed fancy of the patriotic ſecretary, as a routed hoſt, ſcattered and diſperſed by that political ſorcerer, the Vice-Preſident, how was it poſſible to reſiſt the heroic, the chivalrous deſire, of erecting for them ſome magic ſtandard of orthodoxy, ſuch as Tom Paine, and endeavouring to *rally* them round it, for their mutual protection and ſafety.

In ſo glorious a cauſe, the conſiderations—that a citizen of the United States had written, in a foreign country, a book, containing ſtrictures on the government of that country, which were regarded by it as *libellous and ſeditious*—that he had *dedicated* this book to the *Chief Magiſtrate* of the Union—that the *republication* of it, *under the auſpices of the ſecretary of ſtate,* would wear the appearance of its having been promoted, at leaſt of its being *patroniſed by the government of this country*—were conſiderations too light and unimportant to occaſion a moment's heſitation.

Those who, after an attentive review of circumſtances, can be deceived by the artifices which have been employed to varniſh over this very exceptionable proceeding, muſt underſtand little of human nature, and be little read in thoſe arts, which, in all countries and at all times, have ſerved to diſguiſe the machinations of factious and intriguing men.

We have ſeen, that theſe *ſuppoſed hereſies*, at which Mr. Jefferſon affected ſo much alarm, were the opinions diſſeminated throughout the able work of Mr. Adams,—a citizen, pre-eminent for his early, intrepid, faithful, perſevering, and comprehenſively uſeful ſervices—a man, pure and unſpotted in private life—a patriot, having a high and ſolid title to the eſteem, the gratitude, and the confidence of his fellow-citizens—a title which the foul and peſtilent calumnies, which have been circulated through the country, have never yet contaminated.

We have ſeen the baſe arts which have been employed to diſtort his real ſentiments, by ſelecting and diſjointing detached paſſages. We ſhall now ſee whether a leſs unfair proceeding will not convict Mr. Jefferſon himſelf of having foſtered ſome *political hereſies*.

In the diſcuſſion of the charges alledged againſt Mr. Adams, I have animadverted on the unfairneſs of garbling ſentences and mangling expreſſions for the purpoſe of condemning an author's work ; and I have adverted to the practice in the courts of judicature in England, in proſecutions for a libel, where the jury never condemn, " *till they have read the whole* " *work.*"

WILL the enlightened citizens of America condemn an old and faithful ſervant, whom even Hampden ſtiles, " *a patriot of* " *'76,* ' before they have allowed him the means of defence, which are allowed in England to the meaneſt individual ?— Let them read his Defence of the American Conſtitutions, and I ſhall be content to abide by their verdict ;—but let them ſpurn, with juſt contempt, the venomous inſinuations of party.

WOULD Mr. Jefferſon be content to have *his* opinions examined by the rule which has been applied by his partizans to Mr. Adams ? Would he acquiefce without appeal, in a ſentence of condemnation, which ſhould be altogether grounded on mangled quotations, and partial extracts from his writings ?

THE charge againſt Mr. Adams by Hampden is, that he is an advocate for monarchy and privileged orders ; and this charge is ſaid to be founded on certain expreſſions in his work.

I DO not mean to retort with ſeverity the charge, and accufe Mr. Jefferſon of being at this time, an advocate for monarchy and privileged orders ; but I am warranted in aſſerting, that, without doing any violence to the context, I can produce from his writings particular paſſages, as much in favour. of monarchy and privileged orders, as any paſſages in Mr. Adams's book.

FOR example—In ſpeaking of the impolicy of increaſing the population of the United States, by encouraging the introduction of foreigners, in page 93 of his Notes on Virginia, he obſerves, that foreigners will infufe into our government their ſpirit, &c. ; by waiting ſome years longer, our government will be more homogeneous, more peaceable, more durable. He then adds, " Suppoſe † twenty millions of REPUB- " LICAN Americans, thrown all of a ſudden into *France,* " what would be the *condition* of that kingdom ? If it would " be MORE TURBULENT, LESS HAPPY, LESS STRONG, we " may believe, that the addition of half a million of foreign-

---

† A very curious ſuppofition, by the bye, inaſmuch as there were not at that time, THREE millions of republican Americans in the world. Where, then, was he to find theſe twenty millions ?

" ers to our prefent numbers, would produce a fimilar effect
" here."

Now, it is evident, from the above extract, that Mr. *Jeffer-
fo believed* that a *monarchical* government was the beft fuited
to France, and that fending there twenty millions of *republican* Americans would render France *more turbulent, lefs happy*,
and *lefs ftrong*. If he thought that *twenty* millions of *American republicans* (who arc juftly reckoned the beft republicans
on the globe) would *diforganife* France, and *diminifh* her *happinefs* and her *ftrength*, he muft have been fully perfuaded, that
thirty millions of *French republicans* (who, with all their merits
are certainly inferior to the Americans in the fcience of felf-
government) would produce thofe effects in a much greater
degree.

An opinion, in favour of *monarchy* may then without difficulty be inferred from the foregoing paffage.

In page 126 of the fame work, in enumerating what he
calls the *capital defects* of the conftitution of *Virginia*, he complains bitterly of the conftruction of the *fenate*, as not being
fufficiently *ariftocratic*, although the members are chofen for
four years, as long a period as in any ftate in the Union, except Maryland. But he complains, becaufe the *fenate*, and
the electors of the fenate, do not conftitute a *different intereft*
from the reft of the community. He fays, " The *fenate* is,
" by its conftitution, *too homogeneous* with the houfe of dele-
" gates ; being chofen by the fame electors, at the fame time,
" and out of the fame *fubjects*, the choice falls of courfe, on
" *men of the fame defcription*. The purpofe of eftablifhing dif-
" ferent houfes of legiflation is, to *introduce* the *influence of dif-
" ferent interefts* or *different principles*. In fome of the Ameri-
" can ftates the delegates and fenators are fo chofen, as that
" the firft reprefent the *perfons*, and the fecond the *property* †
" of the ftate ; but, with us, *wealth* and *wifdom* have an
" *equal* chance for admiffion into both houfes. We do not
" therefore derive, from the feparation of our legiflature into
" two houfes, thofe *benefits* which a *proper complication of prin-
" ciples* is capable of producing, and thofe which *alone* can
" compenfate the evils which may be produced by their dif-
" fentions."

Now can there be a ftronger recommendation of *ariftocracy
and privileged orders* than we find in this paffage ? He wifhes to
fee introduced into the conftitution of Virginia, an INFLUENCE

---

† There is nothing of the kind in any of the American conftitutions; the affertion
is untrue.

of INTERESTS different from those of the mass of the *subjects*
(as he calls the people) and to establish a permanent con-
stitutional separation of two *orders* of people, on *different principles* ; one to be represented by the Senate, the other by
the Delegates ; he wishes to have WEALTH altogether represented in the Senate, and *wisdom* in the other house, and
laments that *wisdom* has an *equal* chance with *wealth* of admis-
sion into the Senate. What is all this but an establishment of
privileged orders and of an *aristocracy* of the rankest kind ?
The *wealth* of the state is to constitute a SEPARATE CLASS,
to be represented EXCLUSIVELY in a Senate, which is to be
organized on *different principles*, and which is to *maintain an
influence of different interests* from those of the rest of the society. Such a body, having an equal participation of the le-
gislative power with the poorer representatives of the poorer
class, would soon crush the other branch and usurp all power; it would soon erect itself into an *hereditary* aristocracy,
like that of *Venice*. Is there any distinction, except in names,
between a *privileged order*, and a distinct class of men, enabled
by their possession of wealth and exclusive representation in a
branch of the legislature to maintain a separate influence in the
state ? What in fact is a privileged order but a separate class of
men, possessing by law exclusive privileges ? What did Mr. Jefferson wish to establish in Virginia ?—" a separate and *privileged*
" *class*, composed of the *wealthy*, possessing by law an *influence*,
" different from that of the rest of the people, and *exclusively* re-
" presented in the Senate ?" Now I defy his champions to produce any fragment from Mr. Adams's book, so pointedly in favor
of privileged orders, as applicable to the United States, as the
foregoing quotation.

AN *aristocracy of wealth* being thus established by law, *titles*
would follow of course ; it matters little whether such a Virginia senator, as Mr. Jefferson wished to create, was to be stiled
honorable, or *illustrious*, the title of a Venetian senator ; the latter would most probably be annexed ; for we find even *Hampden*, while extolling the republican character of his patron, so
far forgets himself as to stile him the *illustrious* *Jefferson* ; he
presently after speaks of his *wealth ;* thus connecting his *riches*
with his *illustrious* character, as though he had just been reading
his plan of a *Virginia house of nobles*.

WILL it be now denied that even Thomas Jefferson, that pro-
totype of republicanism, has in his writings, countenanced doctrines favorable to monarchy and aristocracy ; that he has, in
this respect, at least as much forfeited his title to the public
favor, as Mr. Adams, and that henceforward his partizans, if
they have any sense of decency, ought to be silent on this subject ?

It has been stated, that the object of Mr. Adams's book was to point out the tendency of a *single* legiflative branch to destroy the liberties of the people. His reasoning in favour of a diftribution of the legiflative power into two branches, and the eftablifhment of checks and balances, has been wickedly perverted into a reasoning in fupport of privileged orders. Who has not feen the venemous effufions, and the low ribaldry, which have of late been disgorged from the *Jacobine* prefles againft Mr. Adams's fyftem of checks and balances ? Who would have fuppofed, that *fimilar* reasoning and principles were to be found in the works of Mr. Jefferfon, the *favorite of thofe prefles*, and the very man who had firft founded the alarm againft Mr. Adams's fyftem of checks and balances, in other words, his *political herefies* ? Such however is the fact.

In the Notes on Virginia, page 126, the conftitution of Virginia is condemned by Mr. Jefferfon, becaufe " all the powers " of government refult to the legiflative body." " The con- " centrating thefe, (he adds) in the fame hands, is precifely the " † *definition* of defpotic government. It will be no allevia- " tion that thefe powers will be exercifed by a *plurality* of " hands, and not by a fingle one.—*One hundred and feventy-* " *three defpots* would furely be as oppreffive as *one*. Let thofe " who doubt it, turn their eyes on the republic of Venice. As " little will it avail us that they are *chofen by curfelves* : an " *elective* defpotifm was not the government we fought for ; " but one which fhould not only be founded on free principles, " but in which the powers of government fhould be fo divided " and *balanced* among feveral bodies of magiftracy, as that no " one could tranfcend their legal limits, without being " effectually *checked* and reftrained by the others. '

Now, here we find a very able recommendation of *checks* and *balances ;* and we are told, that we are *not to truft* even thofe whom *we elect ourfelves*, unlefs *checked* by fome other power ; for, if not fo checked, they will foon be converted into *elective defpots*.

Such were the opinions of Mr. Jefferfon, when he wrote his Notes on Virginia. Whether his *fubfequent refidence in France* has effected a total change in thefe opinions, we have not the materials to decide ; thofe we poffefs involve the matter in obfcurity ; for although in his letter to Mr. Madifon from Paris, dated December 20, 1787, on the fubject of the new federal conftitution, he fays, " I like the *negative* given

---

† This concentration might be the eftablifhment of defpotic government, but it is difficult to comprehend how it is the *definition* of it.

to the executive ;" yet, a few years after his return from France, this kind of check was ranked by him among Mr. A-dams's *political herefies ;* and though, in that letter, he feems to approve of the diſtribution of the legiſlative power, by the American conſtitution, into two branches ; yet he, is faid to have been confulted about, and to have approved, the French conſtitution of 1791, which veſted the whole legiſlative power in one branch, and thus, according to his doctrine, eſtabliſhed (or, to ufe his expreſſion, *defined*) an *elective* defpotifm.

THE friends of Mr. Jefferfon, while they hold him up as the quinteſſence of *republicanifm*, affect to be prodigioufly alarmed left the enemies of republicanifm fhould gain the afcendancy in the United States. Nothing can be more prepoſterous than this filly affectation. Thofe who make the moſt oſtentatious parade of it, are known to be characters the moſt anti-republican in their private life, their public conduct, and all their views.

IT is certain, that Mr. Jefferfon himfelf, whatever he might affect, entertains none of thefe fears. In a letter, already re-ferred to, from him, are thefe expreſſions : " The riſing race " (in the United States) are *all* republicans. We were edu-" cated in royalifm : no wonder if fome of us retain that idol-" atry ſtill. Our young people are educated in republicanifm ; " an *apoſtacy* from that to royalifm, is unprecedented and *im-*" *poſſible*." What ground then for thefe apprehenfions ? How muſt every judicious and independent citizen reprobate fuch bafe attempts to miſlead the public, and to defame fome of the beſt characters in the United States ? And of whom are thefe fears entertained ? Of Mr. Adams !—a citizen who, through the arduous progrefs of a long public life, has never been be-trayed into one *act*, which his opponents can object to him ; for, it is to be obfervèd, that, although he has been in public life for near thirty years, *they dare not attack his public conduct,* but are driven to the wretched expedient of criticifing his po-litical fentiments, by mifquoting his writings. For my part, were I a fouthern planter, owning negroes, I fhou'd be ten thoufand times more alarmed at Mr. Jefferfon's ardent wifh for *emancipation*, than at any *fanciful* dangers from monar-chy. *Emancipation* is a *poſſible* thing ; but *apoſtacy to royalifm,* according to Mr. Jefferfon, *is impoſſible.*

I HAVE produced written fentiments of Mr. Jefferfon, which will bear a conſtruction at leaſt as unfriendly to republi-canifm, as any ever affixed to Mr. Adams's works. I will now call on the adverfaries of the latter to produce, from the works of the former, a more glowing panegyric on, or a more affec-

tionate evidence of attachment to, true republicanifm, than is
to be found in the following paffage of Mr. Adams's Defence.
After pointing out, with great ability, the fuperior advantages
of a republican government, he fays, in page 95, " After all,
" let us compare every conftitution we have feen with thofe of
" the United States of America, and we fhall have no reafon
" to blufh for our country. On the contrary, we fhall feel
" the ftrongeft motives to fall upon our knees, in *gratitude to*
" *heaven*, for having been gracioufly pleafed to give us *birth*
" *and education in that country*, and for having deftined us to
" *live under her laws*. We fhall have reafon to *exult*, if we
" make our *comparifon* with England, and the *Englifh confti-*
" *tution*. *Our people* are undoubtedly *fovereign*—All the land-
" ed and other property is in the hands of the citizens—Not
" only their reprefentatives, but their *fenators* and governors,
" are a *nnually* chofen.—There are no *hereditary* titles, honors,
" offices, nor *diftinctions*. The legiflative, executive and judi-
" cial powers are carefully feparated from each other. The
" powers of the one, the few, and the many, are nicely ba-
" lanced in their legiflatures. *Trials by jury* are preferved in
" all their glory ; and there is *no ftanding army*. The *habeas*
" *corpus* is in full force ; and the *prefs* is the *moft free* in the
" world : and where all thefe circumftances take place, it is
" unneceffary to add, that *the laws alone can govern.*"

In this paffage, Mr. Adams goes beyond Mr. Jefferfon in
commendation of democratic republicanifm, for he approves of
the *annual* choice of *fenators*, as in New-England, while Mr.
Jefferfon, not content with a *quadrennial* election of the
fenate in Virginia, wants to inveft that body with *peculiar and
exclufive privileges ;* Mr. Adams rejoices that we have no hereditary diftinctions in America ; Mr. Jefferfon was defirous of
clothing the wealthy clafs of Virginia, with conftitutional, permanent and exclufive privileges, amounting to *hereditary diftinctions.*

HAMPDEN, unable to attack with effect any part of Mr.
Adams's *known* public acts, though fo long in public life, relates
a *fact*, as he calls it, *refpecting* his *public conduct* : " When feve-
" ral important queftions, which had received the fanction of
" the houfe of reprefentatives, have been fubmitted to his deci-
" fion, as prefident of the fenate, upon an equal divifion of that
" body, he has *uniformly* decided againft the opinion of the re-
" prefentatives, which we may reafonably fuppofe to be the
" opinion of the people ! I believe," he adds, " no member
" of congrefs will contradict this fact."

WITHOUT being a member of congrefs, I will undertake to

contradict this fact, and to prove that Hampden's affertion is as falſe, as his reaſoning thereon is abſurd.

As the vice prefident is, by the conſtitution, placed in the chair of the fenate, with a caſting vote, it was intended that he ſhould exercife his judgment, in giving that vote : and whether the meaſure in queſtion, had been approved by the houſe of re-preſentatives or not, he ought not to concur, if his judgment decidedly rejected it.

A *memorable* inſtance may however be adduced, where Mr. Adams gave the caſting vote in the affirmative, in refpect to a meaſure which had paffed the houſe of repreſentatives : it was in the feffion of 1790 ; a vote had paffed the repreſenta-tives for removing Congreſs from New-York ; this had been a ſubject of much conteſt, and the vote was conſidered as a great triumph by the ſouthern members, becauſe it was an important ſtep towards fixing the feat of government in a more ſouthern · ſituation : the fenate were eqnally divided on the queſtion, Mr. Adams decided in the affirmative, and on being aſked by fome eaſtern member (who complained that fuch vote had been inju-rious to the eaſtern ſtates) why he had voted in the affirmative, he made the following reply, which was related to me by a member of the fenate who heard him, " That whenever the fenate ſhould be equally divided, on a ſubject, which had paffed the houſe of repreſentatives, he ſhould always *vote with the houſe,* unleſs he had very clear and convincing reaſons in his judgment againſt it.

The two houſes differing afterwards as to the place, whether Philadelphia or Baltimore, nothing was then done ; but the *refidence bill* paffed foon after. Here then is a *fact*, which completely difproves Hampden's affertion, and which ought to remove from the minds of our fellow-citizens every degree of credit to the affertions of this malignant writer, and others of a fimilar ſtamp, who do not accompany their accuſations with proof.

And I have not only deſtroyed Hampden's charge againſt Mr. Adams, of having *uniformly* voted in the fenate againſt the opinion of the repreſentatives, but have produced a ſtrong inſtance to ſhew that Mr. Adams had laid it down as a rule, to vote with the repreſentatives, in cafes of equal diviſion in the fenate, unleſs his judgment was very clearly and ſtrongly con-vinced that he ought to vote differently.

I could produce fome other inſtances of his having pur-fued that line, but one pointed cafe was fufficient to convict

Hampden of a falfe affertion. The refutation of this, and the preceding charges, fo pofitively made, will put the good ci tizens of this country on their guard againft fimilar charges produced againft Mr. Adams.

Where did Hampden find the fact? If in the journals of the fenate, let him produce the cafes, for they are all ftated in the journals : if thofe be reforted to, I am convinced as many inftances can be found where Mr. Adams voted on the one fide as on the other. Hearfay and mere report are not fufficient grounds of condemnation before the enlightened tribunal of the public. It feems to be the peculiar characteriftic of thofe, who ftile themfelves in this country, the *exclufive patriots*, the *true democrats*, to build up their own reputation on the ruin of their adverfaries, and to fupport their importance by inceffant detraction and the moft barefaced falfehoods. But however they may have hitherto maintained fome little confequence with a few uninformed citizens, the light of truth will ere long difpel the baneful mifts of calumny, with which they have enveloped the beft men among us, and make thefe defigning hypocrites fkulk back into their native obfcurity.

If Mr. Adams has fometimes voted differently from the reprefentatives, it is to be fairly prefumed that his judgment fo directed him, nor can it be inferred that in fuch cafes he was clearly on the wrong fide ; when fo enlightened a body as the fenate are equally divided, the queftion will be allowed to be a nice one, and although it may have been carried in the reprefentatives, yet the majority there may have been fmall, which indeed we know to have been ufually the cafe in important queftions.

It by no means follows, as Hampden fuppofes, " that the " opinion of the reprefentatives muft be always the opinion of " the people." If fo, all the fenates, all the qualified negatives of the executives ought to be abolifhed : the affertion is a libel on the American conftitutions, and a fevere cenfure on Mr. Jefferfon's doctrine, for he calls the mere will of the reprefentatives (unchecked by the executive or fenate) an *elective tyranny*, the *very definition of defpotifm*. If Mr. Adams *ought*, againft his decided judgment, to vote with the reprefentatives on every equal divifion of the fenate, that body would foon be a fuperfluous member of the conftitution, and the conftitution, now fo much admired, converted into an elective defpotifm.

The univerfal eftablifhment of fenates in the United States, proves however, that our citizens think differently from Hampden on this fubject, and their frequent approbation of the conduct of the fenates and executives, in refifting the will of the reprefentatives (frequently the momentary will of a wicked faction,) proves that they do not always confider their will as the opinion of the people. No act of the Prefident's whole life has been more grateful to the citizens of America, or has added more to the luftre of his fame, than his refifting the will of the reprefentatives on the late call for papers, which is now viewed throughout the union in its true light, as a meafure of party, merely defigned to anfwer certain views.

HAMPDEN's reafoning is as falfe as his FACT : he firft affumes a fact, inconfiftent with truth, and then argues on it on principles, totally inconfiftent with the principles of the conftitution and of public freedom, and in direct oppofition to the principles of his friend, Jefferfon.

AMONG the other merits of Mr. Jefferfon, as ftated by Hampden, we find " his attachment to the CIVIL and RELIGIOUS rights of his fellow-citizens :" for the proof, we are referred to his *writings* and PUBLIC CONDUCT.

WE have feen a few fpecimens of his writings ; from them we may infer a pretty ftrong difpofition to entrench on fome of the civil rights of his fellow-citizens, particularly in his project of a fenate, which would undoubtedly, on his plan, eftablifh an *ariftocracy*, very injurious to the rights of the *poor clafs* of his fellow-citizens.

BUT the proof of a fteady attachment to the civil rights of one's fellow-citizens ought not to reft merely on *writings* ; this attachment ought to be evinced by *public conduct*, by *action*, and in *times of danger ;* then the hazarding of *perfonal fafety* for the prefervation of our civil rights is the higheft teftimony of patriotifm. There is no great merit in compofing, in the cabinet, in feafons of tranquillity, effays on civil rights, which are frequently done to obtain popularity, and without any rifk of perfonal inconvenience.

IT appears, however, that Mr. Jefferfon, has generally facrificed the civil rights of his countrymen to his own perfonal fafety. We are told, in a public addrefs, by Mr. Charles Simms, of Virginia, who muft have been well acquainted with the circumftance, " that Mr. Jefferfon, when *governor* of Virginia, *abandoned the truft* with which he was charged, at the moment of an invafion by the enemy, by which great confufion, *lofs and diftrefs accrued to the ftate*, in

E

the deſtruction of public records and vouchers for general expenditures.†

Now here was a period of public danger, when Mr. Jefferſon's attachment to the civil rights of his countrymen might have ſhone very conſpicuouſly, by facing and averting the danger ; here would have been a fine opportunity for him to have diſplayed his public ſpirit in bravely *rallying* round the ſtandard of liberty and civil rights ; but, though in times of ſafety, he could *rally* round the ſtandard of his friend, Tom Paine, yet when real danger appeared, the *governor of the ancient dominion* dwindled into the *poor, timid philoſopher,* and inſtead of rallying his brave countrymen, he fled for ſafety from a few light-horſemen, and ſhamefully abandoned his truſt§ ! !

Again, when the peace and tranquillity of the United States were in extraordinary peril, when it required the exertions and talents of the wiſeſt and braveſt ſtateſmen to keep the federal ſhip from foundering on the rocks with which ſhe was encompaſſed, he, when his aid was moſt eſſential, abandoned the old helmſman ; and, with his wonted caution, ſneaked away to a ſnug retreat, leaving others to buffet with the ſtorm, and if they were caſt away, to bear all the obloquy and public diſgrace which would follow.

How different was the conduct of the ſpirited and truly patriotic Hamilton ? He wiſhed to retire as much as the philoſopher of Montecelli ; he had a large family, and his little fortune was faſt melting away in the expenſive metropolis, but with a Roman's ſpirit, he declared " that, much as he wiſhed for re-
" tirement, yet, he would remain at his poſt, as long as there
" was any danger of his country being involved in war." How different the conduct of the great Washington ? He tells us, that he had reſolved to retire before the laſt election, but

---

† Mr. Leven Powell, of Virginia, alſo ſtates, in his public addreſs, " that when *Tarleton,* with a few light horſe, purſued the aſſembly to Charlottesville, Mr. Jefferſon diſcovered ſuch a *want of firmneſs* as ſhewed he was *not fit to fill the firſt executive office,* for inſtead of uſing his talents, in directing the neceſſary operations of defence, *he quitted his government by reſigning his office ;* this too, at a time that tried men's ſouls, at a time when the *affairs of America ſtood in doubtful ſuſpence, and required the exertions of all* " The Governor of Virginia, during the *invaſion* of the State by a *ſmall* Britiſh force, inſtead of *defending* the Commonwealth at that alarming juncture, voluntarily and ſuddenly *ſurrendered his office,* and at that criſis, his country was required to chooſe another Governor ! Is there any *ſecurity* he would not act *in like manner again, under like circumſtances ?*

§ This charge has been attempted to be got rid of by producing a vote of the Aſſembly of Virginia, after an enquiry into his conduct, acknowledging his *ability* and *integrity,* but altogether ſilent on his *want of firmneſs,* which had been the cauſe of his flight.

It was natural for his friends in the Aſſembly to varniſh over the buſineſs as well as they could, and the danger being paſt, there being no proſpect of his being again expoſed in that ſtation, and his flight proceeding, not from any criminality, but from a conſtitutional weakneſs of nerves, it was no difficult matter to get ſuch a vote through the aſſembly, more eſpecially as the character of the ſtate was no leſs implicated in the buſineſs than that of the governor.

the then *perplexed* and *critical* fituation of the country forbad fuch a ftep. How different was even *Jefferfon himfelf*, when calmly and *fafely* writing his Notes on Virginia, from what he was when called upon *to act* in times of peril ? in his Notes, page 135, in reprobating the propofition made in the Virginia affembly, to appoint a *dictator*, he exclaims, " Was this moved on a fuppofed right in the movers of *abandoning their pofts in a moment of diftrefs ? Our laws forbid the abandonment of our pofts, even on ordinary occafions.*"

WHETHER Mr. Jefferfon *forefaw* the *weftern infurrection*, and either confcious of his want of courage or capacity to act on fo trying an occafion, or of his good wifhes towards *fome* of the promoters of it, we will not determine ; but it is our duty to ftate *fome* facts ; the comments on them will be left to a difcerning public.

IT is certain that Mr. Jefferfon refigned the office of fecretary of ftate in January or February 1794, and that the *infurrection* broke out the July following, having manifefted threatening fymptoms fome months before. Citizen *Fauchet*, of glorious memory, in his intercepted letter, (which caufed the difmiffion of citizen Randolph, alfo of glorious memory, the virtuous author of *the precious confeffions,*) has the following paffage—" Mr. Randolph came to fee me with an air of *great eagernefs*, and made to me the *overtures* of which I have given you an account in my No. 6.—Thus with *fome thoufands of dollars*, the *republic (of France)* could have decided on CIVIL WAR, or on peace ! thus the *confciences* of the *pretended patriots of America* have already *their prices !* What will be the old age of this government, if it is thus early *decrepid !* Still there are patriots, of whom I delight to entertain an idea worthy of that impofing title. CONSUL *Monroe*,† he is of this number : *he* had *apprized me* of the men, whom the current of events had dragged along as bodies devoid of weight : *his friend* Madifon is alfo an honeft man : *Jefferfon*, on whom the *patriots* caft their eyes to fucceed the Prefident, HAD FORESEEN THESE CRISES : *he prudently retired* in order to avoid making a figure AGAINST HIS INCLINATION in fcenes, the fecret of which will foon or late be brought to light."

WE are informed by the newfpapers that *Randolph has been to vifit Mr. Jefferfon*, and has announced his determination to

---

† Citizen Monroe, lately *recalled* by the Prefident from France, *not* I prefume for his *fervices* to the United States, and not at his requeft : poffeffed of a palace in Paris worth formerly 100,000 guineas (and for the purcha fe of which he was abufed in a Paris newfpaper) it is not probable he wifhed to return quite *fo foon.*

ferve, if elected prefident ; he has not yet announced his own determination to return to his former fecretaryfhip, if his friend fhould be prefident : but his *activity in canvaffing for him* leaves no room for doubt, as to his *wifhes and expectations* : it is apprehended, however, by fome of the friends of both thefe characters, that a lete *legal call* on one of them, for the immediate fettlement of fome accounts and *balances,* will prove highly injurious to both.†

Having adverted to thefe two ftriking inftances of Mr. Jefferfon's *abandonment of his truft* at very *critical moments,* I cannot omit the following fenfible remark of Mr. Charles Simms—" Thefe inftances, he obferves, fhew Mr. Jefferfon " *to want firmnefs,* and a man, who fhall once have abandoned " the helm in the hour of danger, or at the *appearance of* " *a tempeft,* feems not fit to be trufted in better times, *for no* " *one can know how foon or from whence a ftorm may come.*"

THOSE who are acquainted with Mr. Adams's public conduct, from the very commencement of the revolution, can bear witnefs to *his firm and fteady* purfuit of his patriotic career, amidft the *profcriptions* of a powerful and enraged government, and the multiplied dangers which threatened him at various periods : his *manly* and independent conduct at Paris in *negociating the peace,* whereby *great advantages* were acquired to the United States, can never be forgotten.

WE are next informed of Mr. Jefferfon's " attachment to " the RELIGIOUS *rights* of mankind," and are referred for his fentiments refpecting religious liberty to his *writings, his conduct,* and particularly to the " *act eftablifhing religious freedom,*" drawn up by him.

HAMPDEN would have acted more wifely, and more conformably, I am perfuaded, to the wifhes of his patron, had he paffed over this *tender* fubject in filence. It was certainly indifcreet to mention *Thomas Jefferfon* and *religion* in the fame paragraph of an eulogy.—*Religious freedom* and *freedom from religion* are now become *convertible* terms with moft modern philofophers, particularly thofe who have been educated in the philofophical fchools of France. Mr. Jefferfon has been heard to fay, fince his return from France, that the men of letters and philofophers he had met with in that country, were generally *Atheifts.* The late impious and blafphemous works of Thomas Paine, reviling the *chriftian religion,* have been much applauded in France, and have been very induftrioufly circulated in the United States, by all *that clafs* of people, who are friendly to Mr. Jefferfon's politics, and anxioufly de-

---

† Edmund Randolph is fued by the Comptroller of the Treafury for a *deficiency* in his *accounts,* while Secretary of ftate, of 50,000 *dollars.*

ſirous of his election to the preſidency. Mr. Jefferſon's friend-
ſhip for *Paine* has been already mentioned ; that *anti-chriſtian*
writer had apartments at Citizen Monroe's at Paris. and ſhould
Mr. Jefferſon be Preſident, there is no doubt Tom would return
to this country, and be a conſpicuous figure at the Preſident's
table at Philadelphia, where this enlightened pair of philoſophers would fraternize, and philoſophize againſt the *chriſtian
religion*, and all *religious worſhip*.—Whatever new lights Jefferſon may have acquired in France, it is certain that he had
naturally very good pre-diſpoſitions on the ſubject of religion.
In his *Notes* on Virginia, page 169, in diſcuſſing the ſubject
of ▓▓▓ous freedom, he makes this witty obſervation—". It
" d▓▓e no injury for my neighbour to ſay there are twenty
" ▓ds, or *no god* ; it neither picks my pocket nor breaks my
" ▓ ; if it be ſaid, his teſtimony in a court of juſtice cannot
" be relied on, reject it then, and be the ſtigma on him." In
page 170, he ſays, " millions of innocent men, women and
" children, *ſince the introduction of chriſtianity*, have been burnt,
" tortured, fined and impriſoned." In page 171, ſpeaking of
the ſtate of religion in Pennſylvania and New-York, he ſays,
" religion there is well ſupported, of various kinds indeed,
" *but all good enough ;* all ſufficient to preſerve peace and or-
" der."

WHICH ought we to be the moſt ſhocked at, the *levity* or
the *impiety* of theſe remarks ? " it does me no injury, if my
" neighbour is AN ATHEIST, becauſe it does not break my
" leg !" What ? do I receive no injury, as a member of ſociety, if I am ſurrounded with atheiſts, with whom I can
have no ſocial intercourſe, on whom there are none of thoſe
religious and ſacred ties, which reſtrain mankind from the per-
petration of crimes, and without which ties civil ſociety would
ſoon degenerate into a wretched ſtate of barbariſm, and be
ſtained with ſcenes of turpitude, and with every kind of atro-
city ? Good God ! is this the man the *patriots* have caſt their
eyes on as ſucceſſor to the *virtuous Waſhington*, who, in his
farewell addreſs, ſo warmly and affectionately recommends to
his fellow-citizens, the *cultivation of religion*. Contraſt with
the above frivolous and impious paſſage † the following digni-
fied advice from that true patriot ; " of all the diſpoſitions and
" habits, which lead to political proſperity, *religion* and *mora-
" lity* are indiſpenſible ſupports. In vain would *that man* (he
" ſeems to point at *Jefferſon !*) claim the tribute of patriotiſm,

---

† Contraſt even an obſervation of *his* own in one of his letters, already referred to,
where he ſays, " the declaration that religious faith ſhall be unpuniſhed, does not give
" impunity to *criminal acts dictated by religious errors*." He then believed that religious error would produce criminal acts ! and yet *religious error does no injury to ſociety !* abſurd and inconſiſtent writer !

" who should *labor* to subvert these great *pillars* of *human*
" *happiness*, these *firmest props* of the *duties of men and citizens.*
:" The mere politician, equally with the pious man, ought to
" respect and to *cherish* them. A volume could not trace all
" their *connexions with private and public felicity.*

" 'Let it simply be asked where is the security for proper-
" ty, for reputation, for *life*, if the sense of *religious* obligation
" *desert the oaths*, which are the instruments of investigation in
" courts of justice ? And let us, with caution, indulge the
" supposition that MORALITY *can be maintained* WITHOUT
" RELIGION. Whatever may be conceded to the influence of
" *refined* education on minds of peculiar structure, reason
" and experience both forbid us to expect that NATIONAL
" MORALITY can prevail in exclusion of RELIGIOUS PRINCI-
" PLE. 'Tis substantially true, that virtue or morality is a ne-
" cessary spring of *popular* government. The rule indeed ex-
" tends with more or less force to every species of free govern-
" ment. Who that is a *sincere friend* to it can look with indif-
" ference upon *attempts to shake* the foundation of the fabric ?—
" Can it be, that Providence has not connected the permanent
" felicity of a nation with it's *virtue ?* The experiment, at
" least, is recommended by every sentiment, which ennobles
" human nature ; alas ! is it rendered impossible by its vices ?''

WHAT sublime sentiments, what admirable advice ! How
must it sink in our eyes the pretended philosopher, who could
attempt to degrade the Christian religion by charging to it the
murder of millions, who could view with such indifference the
many alarming innovations on the mild and simple religion of
our forefathers ? " There are religions, of *various* kinds indeed,
says our philosopher, BUT ALL GOOD ENOUGH.''

GOOD enough indeed for him, who established and patronized
a newspaper, one object of which was *to revile Christianity !* It
is not forgotten, that the *National Gazette*, published by a *clerk*
in the department of state and under the *auspices* of the *secretary*,
lost no convenient opportunity of making a mockery of reli-
gion†, and vilifying the clergy of the country.

IT is well observed by a modern writer, " that *patriotism*, as
a *moral* principle attaching itself to political society, depends,
like every other moral principle, on its relation to *religion.* The
Creator of man has bound the social to the divine virtues, and

---

† See, among various instances, the 36th number of the National Gazette, where the
belief of a *Providence* is treated as an *impious tenet*. In the time of Robespierre, a
member of the convention who had introduced into his speech the word Providence,
was called to order, by the cry of *Point de Providence*, no Providence.

made our devotion and our reverence to himfelf, the ground work of our duties to our brethren and to our country.''.

THE *act for eftablifhing religious freedom,* in Virginia, (the *neceffity* for which is not very obvious,) has been much extolled by Mr. Jefferfon's panegyrifts. I afk them, what good effects has it produced ? Does religion flourifh in Virginia more than it did, or more than in the eaftern ftates ? Is public worfhip better attended ? Are the minifters of the gofpel better fup-ported, than in the eaftern ftates ?

THAT act, which is nearly all preamble, fetting forth a feries of principles, fome of which are proved by late experience in F____ to be *very queftionable,* has, in my opinion, an immediate t____ produce a total difregard to *public worfhip,* an abfo-lu____ to all religion whatever. It ftates, among other th____, " that ____ ought not to be obliged to fupport even the minifters of ____ own religious perfuafion, and that our *civil* rights have no ____ re dependance on our *religious* opinions than on o____ opinio____ in phyfic or geometry ;'' the act then declares, " tha____ fhall be compelled to *frequent or fupport any re-ligious worfhip or minifter whatever,* and that all men fhall be free to profefs, and by argument to maintain, their opinions, in matters of religion, without diminifhing their civil capacities.''

I WILL not accufe Mr. Jefferfon of having been influenced by *felfifh views,* in getting this act paffed ; but thofe acquaint-ed with *his conduct and opinions* will agree with me, that he has fully *taken advantage* of every tittle of the preamble and enac-ting claufe : he has by his conduct proved his religious free-dom, or, rather, his freedom from religion ; and, by his opini-ons, his right to maintain by argument any doctrine whatever, in matters of religion. Who ever faw him in a place of wor-fhip ? The man who can fay he has feen fuch a *phenomenon,* is himfelf a much greater curiofity than the elephant now travel-ling through the fouthern ftates.

BUT how inconfiftent, not only with truth, but with them-felves, are thefe vifionary philofophers, who are thus always ftriking out fome new doctrine ? The preamble ftates, that our *civil* rights have *no dependance* whatever on our *religious* opini-ons ; and yet it immediately after admits, that *religious opinions may break* out into *overt acts* againft peace and good order ; and yet the letter juft quoted fpeaks of *criminal acts dictated by reli-gious error !*

WHAT a conformity do we find between the fentiments of Mr. Jefferfon, in matters of religion, and thofe of Tom Paine ? Where is the wonder, then, if the *works* of the latter are *circu-lated* with fo much *zeal* by the *friends* of the former ? Tom

Paine has ridiculed the Holy Scriptures, and reprobated public worſhip. Tom Jefferſon has attempted to diſprove the _de-
luge_—has made it a queſtion whether the Almighty ever had
a choſen people,† and has, by _example_ and _precept_, _diſcountenanc-
ed public worſhip_. Such is the Chief Magiſtrate whom the
patriots of citizen Fauchet have ſelected for the United States ! !
Such the kindred philoſophers, whoſe _rew lights_ are to be diſ-
feminated throughout America, under the _auſpices_ of the _Chief
Magiſtrate of the Union ! !_

THE _opinions_ of Mr. Jefferſon, relative to the preſent _conſti-
tution of the United States_, are next in order to be conſidered.

IF he is not _antifederal_, it will not be denied that   r-
tained _very conſiderable objections_ to the conſtitution,   d
that his advice to call a _ſecond convention_, if p   ed, w ld
have prevented our having ever obtained _ſo goo   conſtitut_

SOME of his opinions, relative to the conſtitution, are to be
found in a ſeries of letters, written from Pa , in the years
1788 and '89.. Partial extracts from theſe let   publiſhed in 1792, by a friend of Mr. Jefferſon, as a vindication of
his federaliſm. How far they eſtabliſhed it, will now appear.

IN a letter, dated 20th December, 1787, after expreſſing his
approbation of ſome of the features of the new conſtitution,
which had been generally approved of, and which he could
not well object to, he ſays, " I will now add what I do not
" like : firſt, the omiſſion of a bill of rights, &c. &c. The
" ſecond feature I _diſlike_, and _greatly_ diſlike, is, the abandon-
" ment, _in every inſtance_, of the _neceſſity_ of _rotation in office_, and
" _moſt particularly_ in the caſe of the _Preſident_. Smaller ob-
" jections are, the appeal in fact as well as law, and the _binding_
" all perſons, legiſlative, executive, and judicial, by _oath_, to
" _maintain that conſtitution_. I do not pretend to decide what
" would be the beſt method of procuring the eſtabliſhment of
" the manifold good things in this conſtitution, and of getting
" rid of the bad. Whether by adopting it in hopes of future
" amendment, or, after it has been duly weighed and canvaſſed
" by the people, after ſeeing the parts they generally diſlike,
" and thoſe they generally approve, to ſay to them, " we ſee
" now what you wiſh : _ſend together your deputies again ; let
" them frame a conſtitution for you, omitting what you have con-
" demned, and eſtabliſhing the powers you approved._" Even theſe
" will be a great addition to the energy of your government.

---

† Notes on Virginia, p. 175. " Thoſe who labour in the earth, are the choſen people of God, _if ever he had a choſen people._

" At all events, I hope you will not be difcouraged from other
" trials, if the prefent one fhould fail of its full effects. The
" *late rebellion* in Maffachufetts, has given *more alarm* than I
" think it fhould have done. Calculate, that one rebellion in
" *thirteen* ftates, in the courfe of *eleven* years, is but one for
" *each ftate* in a century and a half : nor will any degree of
" power in the hands of government, prevent infurrections.
" *France*, with all its defpotifm, and two or three hundred
" thoufand men in arms, has had three infurrections in the
" three years I have been here ; in every one of which, greater
" numbers were engaged than in Maffachufetts, and a great deal
" ▓▓▓ blood fpilt. Compare again the *ferocious* depredations
" ▓▓▓ infurgents, with the *order*, the moderation, and the
" ▓▓▓-extinguifhment of ours." In another letter, of
" ▓▓88, he fays, " I am glad to hear the new confti-
" ▓▓▓ived with favour : I fincerely wifh, that the
" ▓▓▓ntions may receive, and the *four laft reject* it.
" ▓▓▓ll fecure it *finally*, while the latter will OBLIGE
" t▓▓▓ a declaration of rights, in order to COMPLETE
" THE UNION." In another of the 31ft fame month, he fays,
" The abandoning the principle of *neceffary rotation* in the *fe-
" nate*, has, I fee, been difapproved by *few*—in the cafe of the
" *Prefident*, by *none*. I readily, therefore, fuppofe *my opinion
" wrong*, when oppofed by the majority, as in the former in-
" ftance, and the totality, as in the latter." In a letter of the
18th November, 1788, he fays, " As to the bill of rights,
" however, I ftill think it fhould be added ; and I am glad to
" fee, that three ftates have at length confidered the perpetual
" re-eligibility of the Prefident, as an article which fhould be
" amended. I fhould *deprecate* with you, indeed, the meet-
" ing of a *new convention*."

, How far thefe extracts were *altered* or *mutilated*, is liable to
queftion, from the manner of their appearance. It is obferva-
ble, that the extract of the letter of the 6th July, though it was
intended as part of the one which is mentioned in the debates of
the Virginia convention, does not anfwer to the defcription
given of it by Mr. Pendleton, who profeffes to have feen it ? for
he exprefsly ftates, with regard to that letter, that Mr. Jefferfon, after having declared his wifh, refpecting the iffue of the
deliberations upon the conftitution, proceeds to *enumerate the a-
mendments which he wifhes to be fecured.* The extract which was
publifhed, fpeaks only of a *bill of rights*, as the effential amendment to be obtained by the rejection of four ftates, which by
no means agrees with the account given of it by Mr. Pendleton.

Such neverthelefs as they are, thefe extracts fully prove,
that Mr. Jefferfon advifed the people of Virginia *to adopt the*

conftitution or *not* to adopt it *upon a* CONTINGENCY ; and that he was OPPOSED to it *in fome of its moft* IMPORTANT *features*, fo much fo, as, at firft, to DISCOUNTENANCE *its* ADOPTION *altogether, without previous amendments.* He GREATLY DISLIKED the abandonment of the principle of *neceffary rotation* in *every office*, and *moft particularly* in the cafe of *Prefident :* he wifhed the principle of rotation to extend not only to the executive, but to the other branches of the government, to the fenate, at leaft, as is explained in a fubfequent letter. This objection goes to the VERY STRUCTURE of the government, in a very IMPORTANT ARTICLE, and while it juftifies the affertion that he was oppofed to the conftitution, in fome of its *moft ——— ——t features*, it is a fpecimen of the VISIONARY SYSTEM ——— —— of its author. Had it been confined to the of——— ——— magiftrate, it might have pretended to fome li—— ——— ; by being extended to other branches of the go———iment, —f- fumes a different character, and evinces a min— —one to *projects*, which are *incompatible with the principles of fta—— goverment*, and difpofed to multiply the *outworks*, while it —— —e *citi- del* weak and *tottering.*

ANY perfon acquainted with *his manner*, and with the force of terms, will not hefitate to pronounce that he wifhed to re- commend a recurrence to a *fecond convention.* The pains which he takes, while recommending a fecond convention, to remove the *alarm* naturally infpired by the *infurrection* in Maffachufetts, which had recently occurred, are a ftrong confirmation of this opinion.

IT is not eafy to underftand what other object his comments on that circumftance could have, but to *obviate* the *anxiety* which it was calculated to infpire in the people for an *adeption* of the conftitution, without a previous attempt to amend it, and to remove all apprehenfion of *internal convulfions* from the dangerous experiment of a fecond convention.

WE cannot avoid remarking, by the way, that thofe com- ments afford a curious and *characteriftic* fample of *logic* and calcu- lation. " One rebellion in *thirteen* ftates, in the courfe of *ele- ven* years, is but *one* for *each* ftate in a century and a half," while *France*, it feems, had had three infurrections in three years. In the latter inftance, the *fubdivifions* of the entire na- tion are confounded in *one mafs* ; in the former, the *fubdivifions* are the *ground of calculation ;* and thus a *miferable fophifm* is gravely made a bafis of political *confolation* and conduct ; for, according to the data ftated, it was as true that the *United States* had had one rebellion in eleven years, endangering their *common fafety* and welfare, as that *France* had had three infurrec- tions in three years.

Thus it appears from the *very documents pr duced in exculpation* of Mr. Jefferson, that he in fact *discountenanced* in the first inftance, *the adoption* of the conftitution in its primitive form, favouring the idea of an attempt at previous amendments *by a second convention ;* which was *precifely* the *line of policy* followed by all thofe who were at that time denominated ANTIFEDERAL, and who have generally fince retained their original ENMITY againft the conftitution. As to thofe letters of Mr. Jefferfon, which are *fubfequent* to his *knowledge* of the *ratification* of the conftitution by the *requifite number of ftates*, they prove nothing, but that he was willing to *play the politician.* They can at beft only be received as expedient acts of *fubmiffion* ▉pinion of the majority, which he profeffed to believe ▉, (refigning to it, with all poffible humility, not only ▉, but his judgment,) not as marks of *approbati-*

It will be remarked that there was no want of *verfatility* in his ▉pinions, they kept pace tolerably well with the progrefs of the bufinefs, and were quite as *accommodating* as circumftances feemed to require.† On the 31ft July 88, when the *adoption* of the conftitution was *known*, the *various and weighty* objections of March 1787, had refolved themfelves into the *fimple* want of a bill of rights. In November following, on the ftrength of the authority of three ftates (overruling, in that inftance, the maxim of implicit deference for the opinion of the majority) that *lately folitary* defect acquires a companion, in a *revival* of the *objection* to the re-elegibility of the Prefident. And *another convention*, which had appeared no very alarming expedient, *while the entire conftitution was in jeopardy*, became an object to be *deprecated*, when *partial* amendments to an *already eftablifhed conftitution* were alone in queftion.

From the fluctuations of fentiment, which appear in the extracts that have been publifhed, it is natural to infer, that had the whole of Mr. Jefferfon's correfpondence on the fubject been given to the public, much greater diverfities would have been difcovered.—But in order to determine with accuracy whether or not Mr. Jefferfon was a friend to the conftitution, we fhould refer to his opinions, while the RESULT was, DOUBTFUL, and not to his opinions, when, after its adoption, his *ftation* and love of popularity made it EXPEDIENT to acquiefce in the will of the majority.

It appears, from the debates in the convention of Virginia, that *Patrick Henry*, at that time the champion of the *antifederal* party in Virginia, *quoted Mr. Jefferfon's opinion, as an*

---

† The Minifter at Paris, with his wonted *political fagacity*, might well calculate, that the *nine* adopting States (in Congrefs) would foon *recall* an antifederalift.

AUTHORITY *for* REJECTING *the conſtitution.* Mr. Pendleton attempted to *explain away* Mr. Jefferſon's opinion ; he ſtated it
to be " a wiſh that the *firſt nine conventions* might accept the
" conſtitution, becauſe it would ſecure the *good* it contained,
" and that the *four laſt might refuſe* to accept *till* they COM-
" PELLED the others to accept certain amendments." Mr.
Henry replied, " the gentleman has endeavoured to *explain*
" Mr. Jefferſon's opinion, *into* an advice to adopt. He wiſh-
" es nine ſtates to adopt, and that four ſtates may be found
" ſomewhere to rejeꞇ it. Now, *if we purſue his advice,*
" what are we to do ? To prefer form to ſubſtance ? For give
" me leave to aſk, what is the SUBSTANTIAL PART____is
" counſel ? It is, that *four* ſtates ſhould REJECT : the____
" that, from the moſt authentic accounts, New-H____
" will adopt it ; where then will four ſtates be fou____
" *if we adopt it ?*"

What ſays *Mr. Madiſon* in reply to this—*Is it come to*
" *this then that we are not to follow our own reaſon ?* I it pro-
" per to adduce the opinions of reſpeꞇable men, n within
" theſe walls ? If the opinion of an important charaꞇer were
" to weigh on this occaſion, could we not adduce a charaꞇer
" equally great ON OUR SIDE ? Are we who (in the gentle-
" man's opinion) are not to be guided by an *erring* world,
" now to SUBMIT to the OPINION *of a citizen beyond the at-*
" *lantic ?* I believe, that *were* that gentleman now on this
" floor, *he would be* for the adoption of this conſtitution ; I
" wiſh *his name had never been mentioned ;* I wiſh every thing
" ſpoken here relative to *his opinion,* may be SUPPRESSED, if
" our debates ſhould be publiſhed. I am in ſome meaſure ac-
" quainted with his ſentiments on this ſubjeꞇ ; *it is not right for*
" *me to* UNFOLD *what he has informed me ; but,* I will venture
" to aſſert that *the clauſe now diſcuſſed* is not objeꞇed to by
" him."

IT is obſervable that Mr. Madiſon neither advocates the accuracy of Mr. Pendleton's comment, nor denies the juſtneſs of
that of Mr. Henry ; his ſolicitude appears to be to deſtroy
the INFLUENCE of what he impliedly *admits to be the opinion*
of Mr. Jefferſon, to preſs out of ſight the authority of that
opinion, and to get rid of the ſubjeꞇ as faſt as poſſible.

HE confeſſes a knowledge of Mr. Jefferſon's ſentiments,
but *prudently avoids diſcloſure,* wrapping the matter in a my-
ſterious reſerve. Enough however is ſeen to juſtify the concluſion, that if Mr. Jefferſon's advice had prevailed, Virginia,
North-Carolina, New-York and Rhode-Iſland, would have
then *thrown themſelves* OUT OF THE UNION. And whether,

in that event, they would have been at this day *re-united* to it, or whether there would be now *any union at all*, is happily a fpeculation which need only be purfued, to derive from it the pleafing reflections, that *the danger was wifely avoided, by not purfuing Mr. Jefferfon's advice.*

WE may now fafely pronounce that, while the conftitution was DEPENDING before the people of this country, for their confideration and decifion, Mr. Jefferfon was OPPOSED *to it in fome of its* MOST IMPORTANT FEATURES, that he wrote his objections to fome of his friends (leading and *influential* men) in Virginia, and *at firft, went fo far as to* DISCOUNTENANCE ITS ▓▓▓▓▓TION, tho' he *afterwards*, finding it received in the United States *with favor, recommended it* on the ground of expediency, in certain CONTINGENCIES.

IT may be added, that fome of his *objections*, which went to the VERY STRUCTURE of the PRINCIPAL *parts of the government*, have not been REMOVED by the amendments, propofed by Congrefs.

WE have feen that the *firft advice* given by Mr. Jefferfon to the people of Virginia, relative to the conftitution, was *not to adopt* it, but to try a fecond convention ; his *fubfequent* advice was, to adopt or not ON A CONTINGENCY, that is, to adopt if *nine* ftates had not previoufly adopted, to reject, if that number of ftates had previoufly adopted, in other words, to rifque an ULTIMATE DISMEMBERMENT of the ftates in an experiment, to obtain the alterations which HE deemed neceffary. On examination, this advice will be found as pregnant with mifchief to the United States, as it was abfurd and whimfical.

IF the four laft deliberating ftates (particularly if they had happened to be ftates in geographical contiguity, which was very poffible) had refufed to ratify the conftitution, what might not have been the confequence ? Would the *affenting* ftates have tamely fuffered themfelves to be COERCED into the amendments, which the *diffenting* ftates might have *dictated ?* Could any thing but objections to the conftitution of the moft ferious kind have juftified the hazarding an eventual *fchifm* in the union, in fo great a degree as would have attended the advice given by Mr. Jefferfon ? Can it be denied that the perfon who entertained thefe objections was STRONGLY *oppofed to the conftitution ?*

THE opponents of the conftitution (or the *antifederalifts* as they were called) acknowledged *like* Mr. Jefferfon, the neceffity and utility of union, and generally fpeaking, that the conftitution contained many valuable features ; *like* him, they only contended that it wanted some essential alterations, to render it a safe and good government ; *like* him, they *only* wanted a *second* convention, to alter the constitution, so as to remove all the objections which had been made, by what they called the people, but in truth, by a few factious disorganizers or visionary theorists in the several states.

IF Mr. Jefferson's advice was not *dangerous*, it certainly was *ridiculous* in the extreme. According to that advice, the question before a state convention would not have been on the merits or demerits of the constitution, but the only question would be, *in what numerical order the state stood ?* If she were the *ninth* state, then it was unnecessary to discuss the merits of the instrument ; it must be *adopted* at all events ; but if she happened to be the *tenth*, it must then be *rejected* at all events, without any discussion. It would have been simply necessary to have ascertained, how many states had adopted, which *fact* being known, the *adoption* or *rejection followed of course ;* and though in other cases, it should seem that the more states had adopted a measure, the stronger would be the recommendation, as an evidence of the approbation of the people, yet in this case, the ingenious Jefferson, reversed the rule, and the more states had adopted, the *less* credit ought it to have with the remainder.

BUT when this very sage advice was given, it happened never to occur to its author, that two conventions might be in session at the same time, and that either of them, by its adoption, would make the *ninth :* what was to be done in this dilemma ? if his advice was proper for Virginia, it was proper for *all* the other states, how would they settle the etiquette, which was to adopt without amendments, and which was to reject, to obtain them ? It would have required conferences and negociations, in which not a syllable would have been said, respecting the merits of the constitution, but the whole discussion would have turned on, which ought to adopt, to complete the magical number, *nine.*

If the contest had occurred between a large and a small state, Virginia and Delaware, for instance, the dispute indeed might easily have been settled ; Virginia would say, do you adopt, and we'll drive them into amendments : little Delaware would not contend with the ancient dominion : But a serious difficulty would have arisen, had the contest been between Virginia and Pennsylvania, and both were determined to adopt or reject : if no *compact* could have been concluded between them, I cannot see how Mr. Jefferson's scheme could have operated : if both refused to adopt, there would not have been the *magic* number ; if both determined to adopt, then *ten* states would have adopted, and no amendments obtained.

And all this, thought Mr. Jefferson, might be accomplished with ease, and *without schism !* Suppose the *four largest states,* Virginia, Pennsylvania, Massachusetts, and New-York, had *rejected* the constitution, and *insisted* upon all the amendments which their several conventions required; is it probable that the other nine states would, without a struggle, have relinquished their opinions, and been *brow beat* into a string of amendments, which they, in accepting the constitution, had deemed frivolous, unnecessary or dangerous ? or on the other hand, had the *four smallest states* withheld their consent, in order to coerce the nine others into amendments, is it likely the latter would have been swayed, by any apprehensions, to alter a constitution, on which they had rested their hopes of future happiness ?

In reviewing the sentiments of Mr. Jefferson, respecting the constitution, we are compelled to ascribe the contradictions and absurdities they discover, to a natural unsteadiness of principle, on the subject of government, and to a disposition, which is very manifest, to please both parties, uncertain for a time, which would preponderate. Thus *his* opinions, like some law cases, were often quoted by *both sides.* At the first appearance of the constitution, he had very *serious objections* to it—and *recommended another convention*—when he found that it was likely to be adopted, his objections diminished, and he advised the adoption by nine states—when he found that the constitution was a favorite with the people, then his objections nearly vanished, and he was content that *Congress*† should recommend amendments when they should be found necessary, he *deprecated another convention.*

If, at the latter stage of the business, he found it *expedient* to acquiesce in the will of the majority, it remains to enquire, whether he has, since the operation of the federal government, continued his acquiescence, or whether, finding in this country, on his return from France, a *party,* unfriendly to that government and to the constitution, from which it emanated, his former enmity has not broke out again, and displayed itself in hostile acts, too conspicuous to have escaped notice and censure.

To prove that Mr. Jefferson has been for many years a determined opponent of the federal constitution and of the measures which have flowed from it, under the administration of Washington, I will now proceed to shew that he was the *institu-*

† In his letter of 28th August, 1789, he says, speaking of a Bill of Rights, the *want of* which he had but a short time before viewed as a *fatal defect,*---" However, if we do not have it now, I have so much confidence in my countrymen, as to be *satisfied* that we shall have it, as soon as the degeneracy of our government shall render it necessary."

tor *and patron* of the *National Gazette,* publifhed in Philadelphia, the *objeA* and *tendency* of which were to *vilify* and *depreciate* the *government* of the United States, to *mifreprefent* and *traduce* the *adminiftration* of it .(except in the fingle department of which he was the head) implicating in the moft virulent cenfure the majority of both houfes of *congrefs,* the heads both of the treafury and war departments, and fparing not even the *chief magiftrate* himfelf ; that in the *fupport* of this paper, thus *hoftile to the goverrment,* in the adminiftration of which he held fo important a truft, he did not fcruple to *apply the money* of that very government.

THIS charge is fupported in feveral ways.

1ft. By direct proof of an OFFICIAL *conneAion* between the *fecrétary of ftate* and the *editor of the National Gazette—a* little antecedent to the *firft eftablifhment* of that paper. †

2d. By direct proof, as we have feen, of the fecretary's being *oppofed* to the prefent government of the United States, while it was *under the confideration* of the people.

3d. By his avowed *oppofition* to the PRINCIPAL meafures which have been adopted in the courfe of its adminiftration.

As to the *conneAion* between the *fecretary of ftate* and the *editor* of the National Gazette, neither of the following facts can or will be difputed.

1ft. That the EDITOR of the National Gazette was a CLERK in the department of *ftate* for foreign languages, and as fuch, received a SALARY *of two hundred and fifty dollars a year.*

2d. That he, became fo antecedently to the eftablifhment of his Gazette, having actually received his falary from the 17th of Auguft, 1791, and not having publifhed the firft number of his paper till the 31ft October following.

3d. That at the time he became fo, there was another character, a clerk in the fame department, who underftood the *French language ;* and that the *editor* of the National Gazette was a *tranflator of that language only.*

4th. That the appoinment was not made under any *fpecial* provifion, marking out a particular clerkfhip of the kind, its duties, or its emoluments ; but under a *general authority to appoint clerks,* and allow them falaries, not exceeding the average of five hundred dollars each.

---

† This *Editor* was well known to be *inimical to good government,* having been a few years before, a writer in a paper, called the Freeman's Journal, the character of which is not forgotten.

5th. That the editor of the National Gazette, *immediately* preceding the eſtabliſhment of that paper, was the ſuperintendant or conductor of a paper belonging to Childs and Swaine, printed at New-York.

These are *the facts* : the *concluſion* is *irreſiſtible* : the *ſecret intentions* of men being in the repoſitories of their own breaſts, it rarely happens, and is therefore not to be expected, that direct and poſitive proof of *them* can be adduced.

Presumptive facts and circumſtances muſt afford the evidence, and when theſe are *ſufficiently ſtrong*, they ought to decide.

We find the *head of a department* taking the *editor of a Gazette* into his employment, as a *clerk*, *with a ſtated ſalary*, not for any *ſpecial* purpoſe, which could not have been accompliſhed otherwiſe ; for beſides his own competency to tranſlate from the French, and his general practice, he had, *at the time*, in his department, a clerk, who was capable of performing the *very ſervice* required, and could, without difficulty, have procured others ſimilarly qualified : nor, from any particular neceſſity ariſing from a too limited allowance, or any other cauſe ; for he had it in his power to allow an adequate compenſation to a character who might have been *regularly attached* to the department.

The very *exiſtence* of *ſuch a connection*, then, is alone a ſufficient foundation for believing, that the deſign of the arrangement was to ſecure an *influence* over the paper, the editor of which was ſo employed. But the circumſtances which attend it, explain the nature of it beyond a doubt. That which has been juſt mentioned, namely, there having been *previouſly* a clerk in the department, *qualified to render the ſervice*, is a weighty one. The *coming of a new printer* from another ſtate, to inſtitute a *new* paper—his having been appointed a clerk in the department *prior* to his removal to this city—his having been compenſated *before* he was even preſent to ſatisfy the *appearance* of rendering ſervice ;—*theſe circumſtances* give a point and energy to the language of the *tranſaction*, which render it *unequivocal*. There, perhaps, never was a more *flimſy covering* for the *penſioning of a printer*. Some *oſtenſible* ground for giving *him the public money* was neceſſary to be contrived. The *clerkſhip of foreign languages* was deemed a *plauſible pretext* : but no man acquainted with human nature, or with the ordinary *wiles* of political intrigue, can be deceived by it.

The *medium* of *negociation* between his friend, the *ſecretary of ſtate*, and Mr. *Freneau*, in order to the inſtitution of his paper, is well known, and documents are poſſeſſed which aſcertain the perſon ; but they are withheld, from particu-

lar confiderations. Thefe are the more readily yielded to, becaufe the facts which have been ftated, render it *unneceffary* to
exhibit them. Thofe facts muft prove, to the fatisfaction of
every impartial mind, that Mr. *Jefferfon* was the INSTITUTOR
and PATRON *of the National Gazette.*

THE complexion and tendency of that Gazette, are fufficiently known. There was no man who loved the government, or was a friend to the public order and tranquillity,
but reprobated it as an *incendiary* and pernicious publication,
and *condemned* with *indignation*, the *aufpices* by which it was
fupported.

IT is unneceffary to add, what is equally well known, that
this *incendiary* paper *expired* about *the time of Mr. Jefferfon's
retirement from office.*

HAVING traced and *afcertained* the *improper connection* which
exifted between Mr. *Jefferfon, while fecretry of ftate,* and the
editor of the National Gazette, it will not be ill-timed to call
the public attention to fome fpecimens of the *fpirit* and *difpofition* by which *that Gazette* was *influenced.*

WE all remember the *alarming fituation* of this country in
the fummer of 1793, when the *Prefident's proclamation,* fup-
ported by *his* energy and *firmnefs,* and by the good fenfe of an
enlightened nation, maintained our *neutrality,* and faved us from
war, in fpite of the perfevering *efforts* of a hoft of *foreign* and
domeftic incendiaries.

MR. Jefferfon is applauded by Hampden for having been
" an *enthufiaftic* admirer of the French revolution, without however *furrendering the independence and felf-government* of America
even to forward that glorious caufe ;" for the proof of which
he refers to the fecretary of ftate's *letter* to Mr. Morris, then our
minifter at Paris, *counteracting* Genet's intrigues and demanding
his recall.—Wonderful forbearance and moderation truly in the
enthufiaftic fecretary *not to furrender* the *independence* and *felf-government* of *his own country,* to forward the glorious caufe of
another ! ! !

BUT the *real* fentiments and wifhes of the fecretary of ftate
are to be looked for in the *publications,* which iffued from a
prefs, of which he was the *inftitutor* and *patron,* and from the
pen of an *editor,* who was *penfioned by him.*

THE *oftenfible* writings of the *mere organ* of the executive
will, *after* the *public* fentiment had become too *unequivocal* to be
miftaken, are not fufficient to convince an intelligent people,
that Mr. Jefferfon was originally defirous of *counteracting* Genet's *intrigues.*

WE find by a recurrence to the *National Gazette*, that after the Prefident iffued his proclamation of neutrality, that Gazette did not ceafe for months to *reprobate* in the moft *fcurrilous* terms *the conduct of the executive*, charging him with the commiffion of an *illegal* act, and with a *flagrant violation* of the *conftitution ;* and that when the Prefident ordered a profecution to be inftituted againft two Americans for *violating the neutrality* of the country by entering on board a French privateer, that Gazette accufed him in the harfheft language, of *cruelly and illegally imprifning innocent* men " for having gene-" roufly forfook their country, to affert the caufe of liberty in " France†."

MR. Jefferfon's tranflator of the French language, after many fimilar attacks, impatient at length of the *tyranny* of the *Prefident* and his *refiftance* to the *will of Genet*, breaks out in his Gazette, of Wednefday, 10th July, 1793, under the fignature of *Juba*, in the following patriotic ftrain—" The mi-" *nifter of France, I* HOPE, will act with FIRMNESS and with " SPIRIT : the PEOPLE are *his friends* or the friends of France, " and *he* will have nothing to *apprehend ;* for, *as yet*, the PEO-" PLE are the *fovereign* of the United States. Too much com-" placency is an *injury* done to *his* caufe, for as every advan-" tage is already taken of France, *(not by the people)* further •" condefcenfion may lead to further abufes. If one of the " leading *features* of our GOVERNMENT is PUSILLANIMITY, " when the Britifh lion fhews his teeth, let *France and her mi-*" *nifter act* as becomes the dignity and juftice of their caufe, " and the honor and faith of nations."

THIS attempt to make a diftinction between the people of the United States and their own government (fo congenial with the attempts then made by the minifter himfelf) and this exhortation to Genet *to difregard the will of the government*, were nothing fhort of a *propofition to transfer all the powers of the executive to a foreign agent*. And fuch was the diforganizing fpirit, which then prevailed, that another Gazette‡, the General Advertifer (now the Aurora) finding fuch doctrines countenanced by the fecretary of ftate, declared, in a piece under the very appropriate fignature of *a Jacobin*, that it was no longer poffible to doubt that the *intention of the executive was to look upon the treaty with France as a nullity*, " and that the government was preparing to *join the league of kings againft France*."

So much were the enemies of the government elated, at that time, with the conviction that the *fecretary* of ftate coun-

---

† See the National Gazette of July 1793.
‡ See the General Advertifer of July 1793.

tcnanzed their views, that they were emboldened to purfue thofe high-handed meafures, which would foon have proftrated our excellent conftitution and placed us at the mercy of a foreign agent, had not *the people* themfelves interfered.

WHEN *Genet*, thus fupported, boldly threw afide the mafk, and raifed the ftandard of oppofition to our government, the people, whofe government it was, came forth from New-Hamp-fhire to Georgia, and with a loud voice, and an impofing afpect, filenced the meddling and crafty foreigner, and put to flight his patricide myrmidons. *Then it was* that Jefferfon found it *expe-dient* to abandon fo rafh an intriguer, and to enlift on the fide of the people ; he, who had greatly difliked the conftitution, while its fate was doubtful, but had apparently approved of it when it met a favorable reception from the people, with his ufual cun-ning and *political fagacity, fupported* the very meafures of the ex-ecutive, when they were found to be popular, which he had, through his agents *refifted* while the *conteft with Genet was du-bious.* Then it was that, like the *friends of the infurrection* of whom *citizen Fauchet* fpeaks, he wifhed to do away all fufpicions of having favored Genet's intrigues, by a parade of great zeal for the independence of our government ; for *thefe men*, to ufe the words of Fauchet, " as foon as it was decided, that the French republic purchafed no men to do their duty, men *about whofe conduct the government could at leaft form uneafy conjectures,* were feen giving themfelves up with a *fcandalous oftentation to its views, and even feconding its declarations."*

IT will be proper, in this place, to ftate fome *facts* and recur to fome *dates*, which will throw great light on this fubject, and fully corroborate the foregoing fuggeftions.

THE *proclamation of neutrality* was iffued 22d *April*, 1793. Genet arrived in the enfuing month in Philadelphia ; and, fup-ported by the democratic focieties, the difcontented and fedi-tious of all claffes, and the *National Gazette*, immediately began his intrigues againft our government. The United States were kept in a ftate of *perpetual ferment and alarm* from the time of Genet's arrival in Philadelphia, till the month of Auguft, when his open threat, " to *appeal* from the Prefident *to the people*," roufed the people to come forward and fupport their Prefident, and thus completely overfet Genet and his adherents, and all their wicked machinations.

Now, Jefferfon's *letter* to Morris was not written till THE 16TH AUGUST ; and the gazette, publifhed under his AUSPI-CES, was filled, from the moment the proclamation was iffued, till the month of Auguft, with *invectives* againft the *Prefident* for iſſuing it, and with *exhortations to Genet* to *perſiſt* in his career !

A few extracts from that letter will aggravate, if poſſible, the groſs miſconduct of the ſecretary of ſtate, in having tolerated ſuch *treaſonable* ſentiments from a preſs, the editor of which was a confidential clerk in his department, and was paid by him with the money of the government, which he was thus openly reſiſting.

He informs Mr. Morris, " that Genet's landing at one of the moſt diſtant ports of the Union, from his points both of departure and deſtination, was calculated to *excite attention*, and that *very ſoon afterwards* the government learnt that he was undertaking to authoriſe the *fitting out privateers*, at Charleſton, *enliſting American citizens* and giving them commiſſions to commit *hoſtilities* on nations at peace with us, that theſe veſſels were bringing prizes into our ports, that the French conſuls were *aſſuming* to hold courts, &c. &c. and all this *before Genet had even preſented himſelf or his credentials* to the Preſident :" He adds, " Genet, not content with uſing our force, whether we
" will or not, in a military line, againſt nations with whom we
" are at peace, *undertakes alſo to direct the civil government* ;
" thus in his letter of June 8th, he promiſed to reſpect 'the
" political opinions of the Preſident, *till the repreſentatives ſhould*
" *have confirmed, or rejected them*, as if the Preſident had under-
" taken to decide what belonged to the deciſion of Congreſs :
" In his letter of June 14th, he ſays more openly, that the
" Preſident *ought not* to have *taken on himſelf* to *decide* on the
" ſubject of the letter, but that it was of importance enough
" to have conſulted congreſs thereon ; and in that of 22d June,
" he tells the Preſident, in *direct terms*, that congreſs *ought* al-
" ready to have been conſulted on certain queſtions which *he had*
" *been too haſty* in deciding, thus making *himſelf*, and not the
" Preſident, the *judge* of the *powers* aſſigned by the conſtitution,
" and *dictating* to him the occaſion when he ſhall exerciſe the
" power of convening congreſs."

From theſe extracts it then appears, that as early as *May*, the attention of the government had been excited to view *with anxiety* Genet's conduct, that he had, even before he was *accredited* by our government, fitted out privateers, enliſted Americans, raiſed a military force, aſſumed juriſdiction, and not content with that, had proceeded as early as June, to undertake to *direct our civil government, dictating to the Preſident* the exerciſe of his powers. And yet, ſtrange to tell, Mr. Jefferſon's tranſlator of the French language, the very clerk in his office, who had *confidentially tranſlated theſe very inſolent letters*, in his newspaper of 10th *July*, publifhed *under the eye* of Mr. Jefferfon, "EXHORTS GENET to aĉt with FIRMNESS AND SPIRIT, tells him that the *people* are *his friends*, that, as yet, they, and not the Prefident, are fovereign, that the *Prefident* is *pufillanimous*, and that Genet has nothing to do but to aĉt as *becomes the dignity of his caufe !*" And ftranger ftill, this clerk thus *openly encouraging* the SURRENDER *of our felf government and* INDEPEND-ENCE TO A FOREIGN AGENT, retained his place as *confidential* clerk to the very man, who makes thefe complaints the bafis of Genet's recall, and the affeĉtions of the very officer, whofe duty it was to punifh fuch treafonable praĉtices !

IN another part of the letter, the fecretary fays, " If OUR " CITIZENS have not been already SHEDDING EACH OTHER'S " BLOOD, it is not owing to the moderation of Mr. Genet, " but to the forbearance of the government." And yet the fecretary foftered within his bofom the ABETTOR of *Genet !*

AFTER this, who will be hardy enough to fay, that Jefferfon did not connive at Genet's praĉtices, while the iffue of his *conteft* remained *doubtful !*—Had he felt the indignation which, at that alarming crifis, fwelled the heart of every independent and pa-triotic citizen, would he not have fpurned from his office, the foul fource of fuch attrocities ?

THE wretched apology offered by Jefferfon's friends, " that he could not, in a free country, controul the publications of that Gazette," is too contemptible to require an anfwer. Could he not difmifs from his office a confidential clerk, entrufted with the *fecrets* of the department of ftate, who was betraying his truft, and *openly abetting* a foreign agent in a *conteft* with the *government of his own country ?* Ought he to have maintained any further *official conneĉtion* with a Gazette, which exhorted the foreign agent to *perfevere* with fpirit in ufurping our govern-ment, diĉtating to the executive, and committng aĉts which muft terminate in *civil war ?*

THIS circumftance is fo ftrongly ftamped with political infa-my, that it can admit of no apology.—It marks the views of Mr. Jefferfon, in *colours* which *cannot be effaced* : it fixes a ftain on his adminiftration, which *can never be wafhed out.*

IT will not now be denied, by any perfon acquainted with the ftate of public affairs at the alarming crifis of which we have been fpeaking, that Mr. Jefferfon was averfe to the Prefi-dent's iffuing his proclamation of neutrality, and that he advif-ed the calling together of congrefs, deeming the proclamation a ftep too important to reft on the Prefident's bare authority.—Whether this advice proceeded from a *fecret* wifh to involve us

in *war*, or from a conftitutional timidity, is immaterial to the
prefent queftion : certain it is, that fuch a ftep would have been
fatal to the peace and tranquillity of America : certain it is,
that Genet, and all the Jacobins of the country, and all the
democratic focieties, were extremely anxious for fuch a ftep ;
and while they refted all their hopes of war on the *convoking of
congrefs*, there was no man, who valued the welfare of this country, who did not then fhudder at the idea of fuch a calamity.—
For had congrefs been convened in Philadelphia in the fummer
of 1793, bringing together all the *paffions* which had been artfully excited in various parts of the Union, finding a *mafs of paffions* ready prepared in the metropolis, *operated on* by all the
wiles and intrigues of Genet, and the *manœuvres* of the *democratic fociety*, congrefs would, moft undoubtedly, have been driv-
en to fome intemperate act, of which war would have been the
immediate confequence.

If it was fo difficult to reftrain a *party* in congrefs from car-
rying *hoftile* meafures in the winter following, when the paffions
had confiderably abated, when the public mind had manifefted
a marked wifh for neutrality, and when Genet's influence was
almoft proftrated, how impoffible would it have been to have refifted them, in the midft of thofe agitations, which convulfed the
whole nation, in the fummer of '93, in the midft of thofe political tempefts and whirlwinds which were then directed by Genet ? The few rational and moderate lovers of peace, inftead of
being liftened to with that attention which their opinions afterwards excited, would have been filenced by the overwhelming
acclamations of a factitious *enthufiafm*, and fwept away from their
ground by the irrefiftible torrent of exafperated paffions.

Well might Genet wifh for the calling of congrefs,† when
he found that he could not *mould* the executive to his views :
well might he rave and threaten, when he found the *advice* of
the fecretary of ftate, on which he had depended, over-ruled in
the council, by the difcretion of the two other fecretaries, and
by the wifdom and firmnefs of the Prefident !

The letters which Mr. Jefferfon afterwards wrote to Genet
and to Mr. Morris, and which have been quoted by his friends
as evidences of his oppofition to Genet's intrigues, prove only,
that Mr. Jefferfon poffeffed political fagacity enough to forefee,

---

† In his letter to the fecretary of ftate (printed correfpondence, page 75.) among
other caufes of *complaint* againft the *Prefident*, he ftates the following : " That he
has deferred, in fpite of my refpectful infinuations, *to convene congrefs immediately;
in order to take the true fentiments of the people*, to *fix the political fyftem* of the U-
nited States, and to decide whether they will break, fufpend, or tighten, their bonds
with France···an *honeft* meafure, which would have avoided to the government much
contradiction and *jubterfuge*.

that had he *after* the public fentiment was fixed, perfifted in
encouraging Genet, he would, like his lefs cunning fucceffor,
have been difgracefully difmiffed from office, and, like him,
ruined in the public eftimation : like the friends of the infurrection when they faw the government ftrong, he therefore
made an oftentatious difplay of " his zeal to maintain our inde-
" pendence and felf-government." It is evident, that Genet
confidered this conduct as a *defection from his caufe*; for in his
letter, referred to in the note, he *complains* bitterly of Mr. Jefferfon's *treachery* and *abandonment.* He ufes, in that letter,
thefe remarkable expreffions : " Befides, fir, whatever may
" be the *refult* of the *atchievement* of which *you* have rendered
" yourfelf the *generous inftrument,* AFTER HAVING MADE ME
" BELIEVE THAT YOU WERE MY FRIEND, after having INITI-
" ATED ME INTO MYSTERIES which have INFLAMED MY
" HATRED againft all thofe who ASPIRE to an ABSOLUTE POW-
" ER, there is an act of juftice," &c. page 70.

HERE Genet complains of Jefferfon's treacheroufly becom-
ing the *inftrument* of his *recall, after* having perfuaded him that
he was *his friend,* and initiated him into *myfteries* of ftate,
which had inflamed Genet's hatred againft the Prefident, and
the reft of the adminiftration ; in fact, after having caballed
with this foreign agent, and by calumnies againft the executive,
excited him to refiftance. Again, page 73, Genet fays to
him, in the language of reproach, " If I have fhewn firmnefs
(in oppofing the Prefident) it is, becaufe it was not in *my character* to *fpeak* as *many people do,* in *one way,* and *act* in *another,*
to have an OFFICIAL language, and a language CONFIDENTI-
AL."

NOTHING further is neceffary to prove, beyond a doubt,
the improper encouragement which the fecretary of ftate had
given to Genet to refift the Prefident's authority ; were any
further proof requifite we might refer to the writings of *Helvi-
dius†,* written in the month of *July* by a *confidential* friend of
Mr. Jefferfon, for the exprefs purpofe of proving that the Prefident had no authority to iffue the proclamation of neutrality,
and inviting the people to difobey it ; we might refer to the
obftructions which prevented the recall of Genet, which did
not take place *till the 16th Auguft,* though he had dictated to
and *infulted the Prefident* as early as *June,* and which obftructions and delay, muft have arifen altogether from the *divifion of*

---

† Thefe writings were fo much fuited to Genet's views, that, in his letter to Jefferfon, above quoted, he fays, " I will join only, in *fupport* of the opinions which I meant
" to profefs, fome Writings which have been publifhed here, fuch as thefe of Veritas,
" HELVIDIUS," &c. Page 72.

opinion which exifted in the cabinet ; to what other caufe can we afcribe the delay of demanding the recall of a foreign agent, who had grofsly infulted the government of the country, from the beginning of June to the middle of Auguft, but to the powerful fupport which that agent found, even in the *department*, where his conduct was the moft notorious, and againft which his attacks had been the moft outrageous?

WHEN finally the meafure of recall was agreed upon, and the fecretary of ftate was at no lofs for materials, on which to predicate it, when the Prefident's opinion, as well as that of the public, became too impofing to admit of further hefitation, then the fecretary, to whom the talent of epiftolary compofition is not denied, produced an able letter, in which he endeavoured to make atonement by elegance and energy of ftile for his previous mifconduct and oppofition.

I SHALL conclude this part of the fubject with the following remarks: 1ft. The circumftance of Mr. Jefferfon's being an enthufiaftic admirer of the French caufe (as Hampden defcribes him to be) is far from recommending him, in the judgment of *real* Americans, to the prefidency. The Prefident of the United States ought to be an *enthufiaftic* admirer of no caufe, but that of *his own country* ; *enthufiafm*, in a politician, is clofely allied to *error* and *paffion*, both of which are the *bane* of good government : but enthufiafm for a *foreign country* leads *directly* to fubfervience and devotion to *foreign interefts* ; a chief magiftrate, *enthufiaftically* attached to France, will therefore foon become a *devoted tool of France*.

2dly. I CANNOT difcern the *merit* in Mr. Jefferfon, of having, as Hampden expreffes it, forborne to *facrifice* the *independence and felf government* of his *own* country even to the glorious caufe of *France* ; what attachment muft that man have to his own country who could, for a moment, confider this, as *meritorious ?* Were the fact as ftated (which I deny, and the contrary of which I have proved) I fhould never be induced to view, as meritorious, the mere forbearance to be a *traitor* to one's country, by facrificing its independence and felf-government to the views of a foreign nation.

IN the preceding pages it has been fatisfactorily fhewn, that Mr. Jefferfon, while Secretary of State, countenanced the intrigues of Genet, till they had proceeded to fuch lengths as to roufe the people to fupport the Prefident, and to compel the fecretary to unite with the reft of the adminiftration in demanding his recall.

THIS has been fubftantiated by various corroborating circumftances and direct proofs.

H

1ft. By the publications in the National Gazette, by a clerk of Mr. Jefferfon, reprobating the Prefident's conduct and exhorting Genet to perfevere in his oppofition, for months after Mr. Jefferfon knew that Genet was refifting the government.

2d. By the obftructions which prevented the recall of Genet, from the time of his firft open act againft the government, till the 16th Auguft, and which could only have arifen from Mr. Jefferfon's oppofition in the cabinet to that meafure.

3d His advice to convoke congrefs, a meafure urgently demanded by Genet, and his oppofition to the iffuing the proclamation of neutrality.

4th. The writings of *Helvidius* againft that proclamation, compofed by a *confidential* friend of his, and quoted by Genet, as authority on his fide.

5th. Genet's charging him with *defection*, after having profeffed to be his friend, and *initiated him* into *myfteries*, which had inflamed his hatred againft the government, and accufing him of having two languages, one *confidential* the other *official*.

6th. His being an *enthufiaftic* admirer of the French caufe.

7th. His being recommended and pointed out by citizen Fauchet, in his intercepted letter, as the man whom the Patriots had fixed on as Prefident, fhewing that Jefferfon was confidered by Fauchet, as a friend to Genet's intrigues, notwithftanding his *official* letter.

WE fhall now proceed to notice fome other features of Mr. Jefferfon's violent averfion to the meafures of the federal government, which will ftill further prove his participation in the views of the National Gazette.

THE friends and advocates of Mr. Jefferfon have made no fcruple to *boaft* of his *abhorrence* of the *leading principles* of the *adminiftration of the finances of the United States ;* and the *National Gazette*, one of the main objects of which was to abufe that adminiftration, in conformity to that abhorrence, went fo far in one of the numbers, as to urge the *neceffity* of a *revolution*, in order to overthrow the whole fyftem of *public credit*.

THE leading principles of our fifcal adminiftration were, that the public debt ought to be provided for, in favor of thofe, who, acccording to the exprefs terms of the contract, were the true legal proprietors of it ; that it ought to be provided for, in other refpects, according to the terms of the contract, except fo far as deviations from it fhould be affented to by the creditore, upon the condition of a fair equivalent, that it ought to be funded upon ascertained revenues, pledged for the payment of interest, and the gradual redemption of principal, that the debts of the several states ought to be comprised in the provision, on the same terms with that of the United States, that to render this great operation practicable, avoid the oppression of trade and industry, and facilitate loans to the government, in cases of emergency, it was necessary to institute a national bank, that indirect taxes were in the actual circumstances of the country, the most eligible means of revenue; and that direct taxes ought to be avoided as much, and as long as possible.

Now, I aver from competent opportunities of knowing Mr. Jefferson's ideas, that he has been decidedly *hostile* to all these positions, except perhaps the last, and that, even in regard to that, his maxims would oblige the government in practice speedily to resort to direct taxes.

I AVER moreover, that his opposition to the administration of the government was not confined to the measures connected with the Treasury Department, but was extended to almost all the important measures of the government.

IF Mr. Jefferson's opposition to the measures which are connected with the administration of the national finances had ceased, when those measures had received the sanction of *law*, nothing more could have been said, than, that he had transgressed the rules of official decorum, in entering the lists against the head of another department (between whom and himself, there was a reciprocal duty to cultivate harmony) that he had been culpable in pursuing a line of conduct, which was calculated to sow the *seeds of discord* in the executive branch of the government in the *infancy of its existence*.

BUT when his opposition extended beyond that point, when it was apparent, that he wished to *render odious* and of course to *subvert* (for in a popular government these are convertible terms) all those deliberate and solemn acts of the legislature, which had become the *pillars* of the *public credit*, his conduct deserved to be regarded with a still severer eye.

WHATEVER differences of opinion may have *preceded* those acts—however exceptionable particular features in them may have appeared to certain characters, there is no enlightened nor discreet citizen but must agree, that they ought when clothed with the sanction of law to remain *undisturbed*. To set afloat the funding system, after the *faith* of the nation had been so *deliberately* and *solemnly pledged* to it—after such numerous and extensive *alienations* of property for full value had been made un-

der its fanction—with adequate revenues, little burthenfome to
the people—in a time of profound peace—with not even the
fhadow of any *public neceffity*—on no better ground than that of
theoretical and *parodoxical* dogmas—would have been one of the
moft *wanton and flagitious acts*, that ever *ftained* the annals of a
civilized nation.

YET pofitions tending to that difgraceful refult were maintained in public difcourfes, by individuals, *known* to be devoted
to the then fecretary of ftate, and were privately *fmiled* upon,
as profound difcoveries in political fcience.

YET the lefs difcreet, though not leaft important *partizans* of
that officer, fpoke familiarly of *undoing the funding fyftem*, as a
meritorious work : Yet *his gazette* (which may fairly be regarded as the mirror of his views) after having *labored* for months
to make it an object of public deteftation, told us at length, in
plain and triumphant terms, that " the funding fyftem had had
its day ;" and very clearly, if not exprefsly, " that it was the
object of the party to overthrow it."†

IT may be juftly then, and from fufficient data, inferred,
that Mr. Jefferfon's politics, while fecretary of ftate, *tended*
to *national difunion, infignificance, diforder* and *difcredit*. That
the fubverfion of the funding fyftem would have produced *national difcredit*, proves itfelf. *Lofs of credit*, the reafon being
the fame, muft attend nations, as well as individuals, who voluntarily and without neceffity, *violate* their *formal* and *pofitive*
engagements.

---

† I find in the Bofton Independent Chronicle, (an antifederal paper) of September,
1792, the following publication :---
Mr. ADAMS,
AS the friends of civil liberty wifh at all times to be acquainted with every queftion
which appears to regard the public weal, a great number of gentlemen in this and the
neighbouring towns. have fubfcribed for the *National Gazette*, publifhed by Mr.
Philip Freneau, at Philadelphia : and it is hoped, that *Freneau's Gazette*, which is
faid to be printed *under the eye* of that eftablifhed patriot and republican, *Thomas
Jefferfon*, will be generally taken in the New-England States.   Q.
In the Columbian Centinel (of Bofton) the following reply appeared a few days after :---
" A Correfpondent in the laft Chronicle, recommends to the people of New-England,
a general perufal of the National Gazette, faid to be printed, &c. Whether this is intended as an avowal on the part of Mr. Jefferfon, that *he* is the *real*, and the imprudent
Freneau only the *nominal* editor of this *chafte Gazette*, the public is at a lofs to determine. The advice is adapted to all who *delight* in the moft violent abufe on a government framed and adminiftered by the people of America, to the honour, dignity, and
happinefs of America ; and all who affect too much learning to have any *piety*, will be
pleafed with the recommendation. The Clergy of the country *vilified, religion* conftantly *ridiculed*, muft afford a rich repaft to *infidels* and *freethinkers*. To deprive us
of all confidence in a government inftituted and adminiftered by ourfelves, and under
the aufpices of which the United States have progreffed from diford, poverty and contempt, to happinefs, wealth and honour, is a tafk worthy the pen of a malignant ftranger, to take from us all truft in that religion, for which our pious anceftors exchanged a
civilized country for the wildernefs, and on which we build our brighteft hopes for happinefs in this and a future world, may afford delight to a man like Freneau : but furely T. Adams ought to be well-founded in his affections, before he brings forward Mr.
JEFFERSON as the *patron* of fuch a Gazette."
Mr. Jefferfon's friends never denied the truth of the paragraph in the Chronicle.

Insignificance and *disorder*, as applied to communities, e-qually with individuals, are the natural *offspring* of a *loss of credit, premeditately* and *voluntarily* incurred.

Disunion would not long lag behind. Sober-minded and *virtuous* men, in every state, would lose all confidence in, and all respect for a government, which had betrayed so much levity and inconsistency, so *profligate* a disregard to the *rights* of *property*, and to the *obligations of good faith*. Their *support* would of course be so far withdrawn or relaxed, as to leave it an easy prey to *its enemies*. *These* comprise the advocates for separate confederacies ; the zealous partizans of unlimited sovereignty in the state governments—the never to be satiated *lovers of innovation* and change—the tribe of *pretended philosophers*, but real fabricators of *chimeras* and *paradoxes*—the *Catalines* and *Cæsars* of the community (a description of men to be found in every republic) who leading the dance to the tune of *liberty without law*, endeavour to intoxicate the people with delicious, but *poisonous* draughts—to render them the *easier victims* of their *rapacious ambition ;* the *vicious* and the fanatical of every class, who are ever found the willing or the *deluded* followers of those seducing and *treacherous leaders.*

But this is not all—the *invasion* of *seventy* millions of property could not be perpetrated without *violent concussions.* The states, whose citizens, both as *original* creditors and *purchasers* own the largest portions of the debt (and several such there are) would not long remain bound in the trammels of a party which had so *grossly violated their rights.* The consequences in experiment would quickly awaken to a sense of injured right, and interest such of them, whose representatives may have wickedly embarked, or been ignorantly betrayed into the attrocious and destructive project.

Where would all this end but in *disunion* and *anarchy*—in *national disgrace* and *humiliation ?*

The votaries of Mr. Jefferson vainly endeavoured to vindicate his conduct, respecting his connection with the editor of the National Gazette, and his opposition to the measures of government, while secretary of state.

In respect to the first, they said, " that Mr. Freneau was recommended by several of his fellow-collegiates, men of high reputation and who were interested in his welfare[*]: and that, to entitle him to the office which Mr. Jefferson bestowed on him, it was merely necessary that he should be a citizen of

† See the American Daily Advertiser of the 13th October, 1792.

the United States, irreproachable in point of morality, and in other respects well qualified to discharge his duties."—It is at once seen that, such an apology, to an enlightened public, is as insulting as was the conduct which it was designed to gloss over.—As well might Mr. Jefferson, should he be elected president, and pension a printer to support his measures, attempt hereafter to varnish over such an act by a like vindication.

As to the second point, these votaries, whose devotion for their idol kindled at every form, in which he presented himself, even deduced matter of *panegyric* from *his opposition to the measures of the government.* 'Twas according to them, the sublimest pitch of virtue in him, not only to have *extra-officially* embarrassed plans, originating with his colleagues, in the course of their progress, but to have *continued* his opposition to them, *after* they had been considered and enacted by the *legislature*, with such modifications as had appeared to them proper, and had been *approved* by the *chief magistrate.* Such conduct, in their opinion marked a firm and virtuous independence of spirit†.

If any proof were wanting of that strange perversion of all ideas of decorum and order, which has long characterised a certain party, this making a theme of *encomium* of what was truly a demonstration of a *caballing, self-sufficient, and refractory temper*, would afford it.

I shall endeavour to state what course a firm and virtuous independence of character, guided by a just and necessary sense of decorum, should have dictated to an officer in Mr. Jefferson's station.

I do not hesitate to reprobate the position, that a man, who had accepted an office in the executive department, should be held to throw the weight of his character into the scale, to support a measure, which in his *conscience he disapproved*, and in his *station had opposed*—or that the members of the administration should form together a close and secret combination, into whose measures the profane eye of the public should not pry. But there is *a very obvious medium* between *aiding or countenancing*, and *intriguing and machinating* against a measure ; between *opposing it in the discharge of an official duty or volunteering an opposition to it in the discharge of no duty*, between *entering into a close and secret combination* with the other members of the administration, and *being the active leader of an opposition to its measures*.

---

† See the American Daily Advertiser of the 10th October, 1792.

THE *true line of propriety* appears to be the following :—A member of the administration in one department ought only to aid those measures of another, which he approves—Where he disapproves, if called upon *to act officially*, he ought to manifest his disapprobation, and avow his opposition ; but, out of an official line, he ought not to interfere, " *as long as he thinks fit* TO CONTINUE A PART OF THE ADMINISTRATION."

WHEN the measure in question has become a *law of the land*, especially with a *direct sanction of the chief magistrate*, it is *his peculiar* DUTY *to acquiesce*. A contrary conduct is *inconsistent* with his *relations* as an *officer of the government*, and with a *due respect* as such for the decisions of the legislature and of the *head* of the *executive* department.

.THE success of every government, its capacity to combine the exertion of public strength with the preservation of personal right and private security, must always depend on the energy of the executive.

THIS *energy* again, must materially depend on the *union and mutual deference*, which subsist between the members of that department, and the conformity of their conduct with the views of the executive chief.

DIFFERENCE of opinion between men engaged in any common pursuit, is a natural appendage of human nature. When only exerted in the *discharge of a duty*, with delicacy and temper, among liberal and sensible men, it can create no animosity : but when it produces *officious interferences*, dictated by *no call of duty* ; when it volunteers a display of itself in a quarter where there is *no responsibility*, it must inevitably beget ill-humour and *discord*.

APPLIED to the members of the executive administration of any government, and more particularly of a *republican* government, it must necessarily tend to occasion, more or less, *distracted councils*, to foster *factions* in the community, and particularly *to weaken the government*.

MOREOVER, the *heads* of the several executive departments are to be viewed as *auxiliaries to the executive chief*. Opposition to any measures of *his*, by either of those heads, except in the shape of frank, firm, and independent advice to himself, is evidently *contrary to the relations*, which subsist between the parties. And a measure becomes *his*, so as to involve this *duty* of acquiescence, as well by its having received *his sanction in the form of a law*, as by its having previously received his approbation.

ONE of the powers entrusted to our chief magistrate is, that of *objecting* to bills which have passed the two houses of congress.

This suppofes the *duty* of objecting, when he is of opinion that the object of any bill is either *unconftitutional* or *pernicious*. The *approbation* of a bill implies, that he *does not think* it either the one or the other ; and it makes *him refponfible* to the community for this opinion. The meafure becomes *his* by adoption ; nor could he efcape a portion of the blame, which would finally attach itfelf to a bad meafure, to which he had given his confent.

SOLID as are thefe principles, the public ear has, notwith-ftanding, been frequently affailed with common place to-pics, and plaufible flourifhes and declamations againft them. However fuch flourifhes may be dexteroufly retailed by the traf-fickers in popular prejudice, thefe principles, founded on politi-cal truth, may, with confidence, be fubmitted to the deliberate opinion of an enlightened and fober people.

IT may be afked—What ? is a man to facrifice his *confcience* and his judgment to an office ? Is he to be a *dumb* fpectator of meafures which he deems fubverfive of the *rights* and *interefts* of his fellow-citizens ? Is he to poftpone to the frivolous rules of a falfe complaifance, or the arbitrary dictates of a tyrannical de-corum, the *higher duty* which he owes to the community ? I an-fwer, no ! he is to do none of thefe things. If he cannot coa-lefce with thofe, with whom he is affociated, as far as the rules of *official* decorum, propriety, and obligation may require, without *abandoning* what he conceives to be the *true intereft* of the com-munity, let him *place himfelf in a fituation*, in which he will ex-perience no collifion of *oppofite duties*. Let him *not cling* to the honours or emoluments of an office, and content himfelf with *de-fending* the *injured rights* of the people, by *obfcure* or *indirect means*. Let him *renounce a fituation* which is a clog upon his patriotifm, tell the people that he could no longer continue in it without forfeiting his duty to them, and that he had quit-ted it to be more at liberty to afford them his beft fervices.

SUCH is the courfe that would have been indicated by a firm and *virtuous independence* of character, that would have been pur-fued by a man attentive to unite the fenfe of *delicacy* with the fenfe of *duty*—in earneft about the pernicious tendency of public meafures, and more folicitous to act the *difinterefted friend of the people*, than the *interefted, ambitious, and intriguing head of a party*.

BUT Mr. Jefferfon clung for *four years* to the honours and emoluments of office, under an adminiftration, whofe meafures he greatly difapproved, and perfeveringly *oppofed*, when a very *perplexed* ftate of affairs, and the *alarming profpect* of *approaching war*, could alone dictate his relinquifhment of a ftation, then too pregnant with *anxieties* to continue an object of defire.